A Parent's Guide to

M&mphis

by Denise DuBois Taylor

ISBN 0-9649821-3-7

Bluff City Books, a division of Contemporary Media, Inc.,
460 Tennessee Street, Suite 200, Memphis TN 38103
www.bluffcitybooks.com

EDITOR ~ *Mary Helen Randall*
ART DIRECTOR ~ *Hudd Byard*
ASSOCIATE EDITOR ~ *Amanda Dugger*
PRODUCTION MANAGER ~ *Cheryl S. Bader*

Printed in Canada by Houghton Boston, Saskatoon.

Table of Contents

MAIN STREET TROLLEY

Foreword

In a parent's world dominated by jam-packed schedules and never-ending homework, family time is a precious commodity. Our hectic lives keep us running hard. It's difficult to stop and just live in the moment with our kids. Yet what are the memories we hold most dear when we think of our family? Probably the simple things, like conversations around the dinner table. Birthday celebrations. The joy of watching our kids totter off on their bikes for the first time. The wonder of their discovery when a frog leaps into the murky depths of a pond. Our children are hungry for us to experience their world, to forget for a time our own clogged agendas, and instead, trade them in for a slow, lazy afternoon of exploring. They yearn for us to go fly a kite — together.

So I'm delighted to introduce Denise DuBois Taylor's book, *A Parent's Guide to Memphis*. As an inveterate day-tripper, I'm always on the lookout for new destinations I can share with my family. But since I don't have time to check them out myself, I rely on guidebooks like this one, fat with ideas that have already been mom-tested. That's where Taylor's expertise shines. As the former vice president of Communications & Public Relations with the Memphis Convention & Visitors Bureau, she's long been in the know about the treasure trove of attractions that make the Mid-South special.

In researching this book, Taylor visited a host of specialty museums, parks, bike trails, and fun centers to learn firsthand the most useful, accurate information you'll need for each locale. (She traveled to nearly all the destinations listed here with one or both of her school-aged sons and husband in tow.) She does a great job describing what you'll find, the highlights and quirks, which attractions captivate the preschool set, and which are better suited to tweens or teens. Her boys' voices even surface through some of these pages, lending an enthusiastic thumbs up to a few of their favorites.

I think you'll find Taylor's roundup of information just what you need to make your adventures enjoyable. She even offers suggestions for good local eats, which can go a long way towards appeasing cranky kids. Whether it's a sleepy county museum or a gem of a nature park, there's plenty here to like. I hope that by using this guide, some of these destinations will become your family favorites as well.

So take an afternoon off, grab the kids, and spend time having fun, together, as a family. You'll be glad you did.

Jane Schneider

EDITOR, *Memphis Parent*

CHILDREN'S MUSEUM OF MEMPHIS

I'M A BABY BOOMER. This means that despite the obvious widening of my posterior, the considerable softening of my upper arms, and the growing supply of color-the-gray rinse, I still feel like a kid and want to act like a kid. This can sometimes be complicated when I am also trying to be responsible for kids. Like my own.

I'm a parental late-bloomer. I inherited two sons when I was 39. (Both are now in college.) Then I had one of my own, at 40.

I try to balance that forever-young enthusiasm so often associated with baby boomers while coming to terms with my being a middle-aged parent. I spend much of my time with young parents, some still in their early thirties, but I also have friends closer to my age who are now grandparents. To put it another way, it's hard to keep up with the Joneses when I know so many of them, and they are all going in different generational directions. Personally, I don't have the time or energy to do it all, not to mention what it would take to figure out exactly what "all" entails. So a simple guidebook like this one can make life a lot easier.

My hope is that you will find this publication to be a concise and useful guide to touring Memphis, Tennessee, and the surrounding area. The attractions and activities have been evaluated, the costs have been compiled, the maps have been drawn. In other words, here's everything but the silver platter — at least, just about everything that was in operation as of the printing date of this book.

Who Am I, and Why Am I Doing This?

Who says I'm qualified to write this book? I do. (And obviously, so does my beloved publisher, Bluff City Books/Contemporary Media.) I am a native Memphian, and my family has lived in West Tennessee since 1826, so I like to think I have a pretty good grip on the lay of the land. Additionally, I'm a parent, the daughter of parents, and I know a lot of parents.

I've had some interesting professional experiences over the years, too — waitressing, scooping ice cream, writing ad copy, voicing radio and TV commercials, professional gift wrapping — even a couple of very brief stints on *The Guiding Light* (20 years and 20 pounds ago), but they didn't do much to prepare me for writing a family-friendly guide book. Other experiences, however, were just what the doctor (or editor) ordered.

I worked in radio for two years before beginning a 12-year tenure as an anchor and reporter at the local NBC affiliate. This job took me all over the Mid-South with assignments behind-the-scenes at major events and attractions.

activities that appeal to them!

For added assurance however, I "volunteered" my 13-year-old son Will as my occasional research assistant, and I can assure you he minced no words in telling me exactly what he thought of each place we toured. There were also opportunities to include the counsel of Will's older brother, Andrew, and for one high-flying adventure in particular, I also recruited the eldest Taylor son, David.

If you are a tourist in the area, a new resident, or a longtime citizen,

> *As much as you like to think your prodigy is a budding Mozart or Mary Cassatt or even a Tiger Woods, be realistic about his or her level of interest. It can be frustrating, but sometimes you have to start with those baby steps before they can enjoy the ballet.*

For more than nine years, I also commuted daily from Channel 5 to the headquarters of Holiday Inns, Inc., where I handled corporate communications. I learned a lot about the travel industry at H.I., which helped me step into my next job as Vice President of Communications & Public Relations for the Memphis Convention & Visitors Bureau (MCVB).

The MCVB was a terrific training ground — and a lot of fun. In fact, they *paid* me to have fun as I escorted people (mostly international media types) to area attractions. I also wrote editorials promoting the city, which qualified me to join the Society of American Travel Writers. I journeyed overseas to meet with journalists, further plugging all that makes Memphis the "Home of the Blues & the Birthplace of Rock'n'Roll."

Frankly though, after 10 years of traveling, I was ready to stay put for a while. I took a position at Grace-St. Luke's Episcopal School as Director of Development. What an ideal spot to get in touch with kids and the

this guide will serve as a handy reference with information on all that makes Memphis and Shelby County worth seeing. And if you want to bring your kids, grandkids, or a neighbor's kids, all the better! Virtually all experiences are best when they are shared.

I Stole Some Good Ideas

I don't have to tell you that traveling with children presents a whole new set of considerations, priorities, and necessities. I took the liberty of borrowing some ideas and helpful hints from other traveling families and added a few of my own to compile the following.

Rules for the Road

BE PREPARED: It never hurts to review any safety rules before a trip or outing. Try to keep water and snacks (like fruit and pretzels) in the car just in case the kids get hungry (and grumpy). Keep extra sweaters and umbrellas in the car in case the weather takes a sudden turn. Once you arrive and start exploring local attractions, design an emergency plan. Discuss with your kids what to do in case someone gets lost or separated (where to meet, whom to ask for help, etc.).

DO YOUR HOMEWORK: Make the most of the outing by learning a little bit about it beforehand. Give your kids a few hints about what to expect or why you think the experience is special. Sometimes it's a good idea to tell them about how long the excursion will take.

SAVE A LITTLE SURPRISE: Don't give it all away. Let them make some discoveries on their own. You want them to participate as much as possible.

KEEP IT SHORT'N'SWEET: Consider the ages of your children and their particular interest levels. Try not to overdo it. No one has fun if too many activities are crammed into one day. The kids get cranky and so do their parents! Pick your priorities and, if necessary, save a few things for another day or even another trip. In other words, be flexible.

COMPANY'S COOL: I know my son always enjoys himself more if he can share the experience with a friend. Oftentimes, more is merrier.

GET REAL: As much as you like to think your prodigy is a budding Mozart or Mary Cassatt or even a Tiger Woods, be realistic about his or her level of interest. It can be frustrating, but sometimes you have to start with those baby steps before they can enjoy the ballet.

∾ DISCLAIMER

While this guidebook contains detailed information and lists of travel-friendly resources, it is not all-inclusive. Some services have been omitted because I have not had direct contact with them and therefore cannot personally vouch for them. This does not mean that they are not professional and dependable. It simply means I have no first-hand knowledge of them.

It is also important to note that every effort was made to ensure the accuracy of information presented here — at least as of the printing of this book, but it is always advisable to call ahead before you set out on your various excursions.

CHAPTER 1

Memphis, Tennessee

Home of the blues & birthplace of rock'n'roll

MEMPHIS CITY SKYLINE

MEMPHIS, TENNESSEE, is mentioned in more songs than any other city in the world. In fact, more than 400 songs at last count. It's a city with an inspiring history and lots of interesting people. But let's face it, while scholars may enlighten you with stories of Memphis' famed and infamous citizenry, the city is best known for its mile-long roster of world-renowned musicians. Memphis continues to foster the talents of great songwriters and performers, blending blues, rockabilly and rock, gospel, rap, R&B, and soul. This is why Memphis is so aptly called "Home of the Blues & Birthplace of Rock'n'Roll."

Still, There's More Than Music To Sing About

A number of years ago, I read an article that listed the top 100 entrepreneurs of the 20th century. Memphis had more people on that list than any other city.

A man named Kemmons Wilson founded the Holiday Inn hotel chain in Memphis, forever changing the way modern families travel. Memphian Abe Plough cared for his customers from head to toe, literally, producing products that ranged from St. Joseph's aspirin and Coppertone tanning products to Dr. Scholl's shoe inserts and Maybelline make-up. Another local, Fred Smith, revolutionized distribution with the introduction of an overnight carrier service called FedEx. AutoZone, also founded and headquartered in Memphis, mastered the concept of do-it-yourself auto repairs. Continental and Greyhound Bus Lines were also founded in Memphis, letting folks see much of the country for the first time, in an affordable fashion. The list of innovators goes on and on.

The world's first drive-in restaurant began in Memphis. On one particularly busy evening in 1905, Harold Fortune, owner of Fortune's Ice Cream and Soda Fountain, decided his shop was way too crowded. He instructed his waiters to go out to the customers' cars and buggies to get orders, then to deliver their food. What a concept!

The first self-service grocery store began in Memphis, too. Instead of having customers ask the shopkeeper for items behind the counter, a man named Clarence Saunders offered aisles of food and other goods within easy reach, with little baskets to carry it all. Thus, the Piggly Wiggly chain was born, and the concept of the supermarket was on its way into the mainstream.

The list of "firsts" is long and varied. Memphis may be known for its vast and lumbering Mississippi River, for hot, humid dog days of summer, for Southern drawls, fried foods and tall tales, but there is no denying that this city is also famous for spawning the kind of originality and innovation that forever changed modern, popular culture.

It's Hot, But That's Cool

Be prepared: Memphis gets hot, and the humidity can be smothering. If you're planning on visiting during the summer months, start stripping now. It is not unheard of to reach 100 degrees with 95 percent humidity (right before the thunderstorm rolls in). Consequently, you might want to curb your tourism ambitions a bit. The kids will never forgive you if you drag them to too many places during the heat of the day. After a few hours in the energy-zapping

Average Fahrenheit temperatures in Memphis:

January 40	May 71	September 74
February 44	June.......................79	October 63
March 53	July 83	November 53
April 63	August...................81	December............44

"BOSS" CRUMP (LEFT) ARMISTICE DAY PARADE

heat, you parents might not feel especially fresh and perky either.

The good news is that fall and spring offer ideal travel conditions. And while the area's winters can be uncomfortable, the cold temperatures are not too extreme. Memphis winters also tend to be short — arriving full force after Thanksgiving and long-gone by March.

A Brief History
A Chronology for the Kids
(*pop quiz optional*)

1514 ~ Indians living near present-day Memphis encounter the Hernando DeSoto expedition.

1812 ~ The New Madrid Earthquake, the strongest ever in North America (perhaps 8.8 on today's Richter scale), is centered north of Memphis, causing the Mississippi River to flow backwards for 48 hours and forming Reelfoot Lake.

1818 ~ Chickasaw Nation signs a treaty ceding West Tennessee to the U.S.

∞ What's New?
1900 The escalator **1902** Air conditioner, neon light, lie detector, Teddy Bear **1903** Windshield wipers and crayons **1904** Teabags and tractors **1905** Albert Einstein publishes the Theory of Relativity (E = mc²) **1906** Cornflakes **1912** Life Savers **1913** Crossword puzzle, bra, and zipper **1920** Band-Aids

1819 ~ Andrew Jackson, General James Winchester, and John Overton found the city of Memphis on May 22.

1857 ~ The Memphis-Charleston Railroad is completed, linking the Atlantic Ocean and the Mississippi River.

1862 ~ A Union fleet defeats Confederate naval forces at the Battle of Memphis, and Federal troops occupy the city.

1865 ~ Nearly 2,000 people (mostly Union soldiers) die in the explosion and sinking of the *Sultana*, America's worst inland maritime disaster. The Memphis Freedman's

Bureau is established to assist African Americans in their transition from slavery to freedom.

1878 ~ The worst yellow fever epidemic in the city's history claims some 5,000 lives.

1905 ~ Fortune's Soda Fountain starts taking and delivering orders from customers in the outside parking lot, laying the foundation for America's first drive-in restaurant.

1906 ~ Overton Park Zoo (now the Memphis Zoo) opens.

1909 ~ E.H. "Boss" Crump becomes the city's most famous mayor, boosted by his campaign song: W.C.

Handy's "The Memphis Blues."

1916 ~ Clarence Saunders, the founder of the self-service grocery store, opens his first Piggly Wiggly in Memphis.

∞ What's New?

1928 Electric shaver and bubble gum **1929** A new drink called "Bib-Label Lithiated Lemon-Lime Sodas" (7 Up) **1930** Scotch tape, the analog computer, Clarence Birdeye's frozen food process **1934** Monopoly **1938** Ballpoint pen **1943** Slinky and Silly Putty **1945** The atomic bomb ends World War II **1948** The Frisbee®, Velcro ®, Wurlitzer jukebox **1952** Mr. Potato Head patented.

1923 ~ The Universal Life Insurance Company, one of the largest African-American-owned insurance companies in the nation, is founded.

1925 ~ The present Peabody Hotel opens to the public. Tom Lee rescues 32 people when the *M.E. Norman* sinks on the Mississippi River.

1928 ~ The Orpheum Theatre opens; its predecessor was destroyed by fire.

1942 ~ The Naval Air Station at Millington is built.

1952 ~ Kemmons Wilson opens the first Holiday Inn hotel on Summer Avenue. Sam Phillips opens the Memphis Recording Service (Sun Studio).

NATIONAL CIVIL RIGHTS MUSEUM

1954 ~ Sam Phillips records "That's Alright (Mama)" by Elvis Presley – and the world embraces rock'n'roll.

1954 ~ E.H. "Boss" Crump, Memphis political leader for 45 years, dies. Elvis Presley gives his first concert in Memphis.

1958 ~ Stax Records, home of "Memphis Soul Music," is organized.

1968 ~ Dr. Martin Luther King, Jr., is assassinated on April 4, at the Lorraine Motel during the sanitation workers' strike.

THE ORPHEUM THEATRE

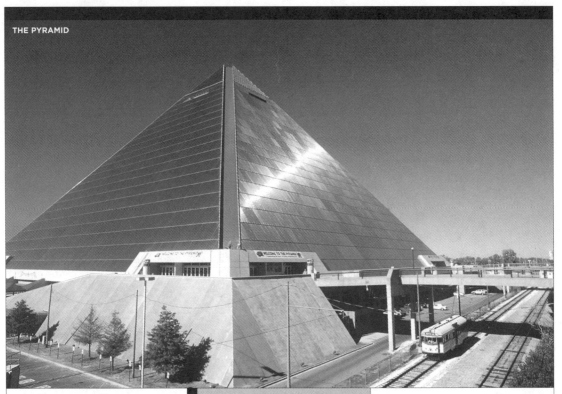

1972 ~ Federal Express Corporation (now FedEx) is founded.

1977 ~ Elvis Presley, the King of Rock'n'Roll, dies at Graceland on August 16.

1981 ~ After being refurbished, the historic Peabody Hotel reopens.

1982 ~ Mud Island, with America's only Mississippi River museum, opens. Graceland is opened to the public as a tourist attraction.

1983 ~ A renovated Beale Street opens, quickly becoming the state's most-visited tourist attraction.

1987 ~ WONDERS: The Memphis International Cultural Series begins with the "Ramesses the Great" exhibition.

1991 ~ The National Civil Rights Museum and The Pyramid arena open. Memphis elects its first black mayor, Dr. W.W. Herenton. Two of best-selling author John Grisham's novels, *The Firm* and

∞ What's New?

1954 McDonald's **1956** Liquid Paper **1958** Laser and the Hula Hoop **1959** Barbie Doll and Spacewar (the first computer video game) **1968** Computer mouse **1971** VCR **1974** Post-It Notes **1979** Cellular phones, Walkman, roller blades **1985** Windows Software **1986** Disposable camera **1990** The World Wide Web/Internet protocol (HTTP) and language (HTML) **1995** DVD

GIBSON GUITAR FACTORY

The Client, are filmed on location in the city. Downtown trolley begins operation.

1995 ~ Memphis' airport becomes truly international with KLM Royal Dutch Airlines' daily, non-stop flights to Amsterdam. AutoZone constructs new international headquarters downtown.

1998 ~ Fire Museum of Memphis and the Peabody Place Museum and Gallery open to the public. A renovated Central Station (and AMTRAK stop) reopens to the public.

1999 ~ The Memphis Rock'n'Soul Museum opens with the Smithsonian exhibition "Rock'n'Soul: Social Crossroads."

2000 ~ AutoZone Ball Park (home to the Memphis Redbirds) opens downtown. Elvis Presley's Heartbreak Hotel opens across the street from Graceland.

2001 ~ Multi-million-dollar Peabody Place Retail and Entertainment

FEDEXFORUM

PEABODY PLACE

Center is completed. Gibson Guitar Factory and Gibson Beale St. Showcase open to the public. Memphis' NBA Grizzlies play inaugural season.

2002 ~ Famed New Orleans landmark, Pat O'Brien's, opens on Beale. Memphis Children's Museum completes multi-million-dollar expansion. The National Civil Rights Museum finishes $10 million expansion.

2003 ~ Soulsville USA: Stax Museum of American Soul Music and the Stax Music Academy open to the public. Pandas (Ya Ya and Le Le) arrive at the Memphis Zoo for a 10-year stay.

2004 ~ FedExForum, home of the NBA's Memphis Grizzlies, opens to the public. The Memphis

Rock'n'Soul Museum relocates to FedExForum from its original home at the Gibson Guitar Factory.

MEMPHIS TOURISM: FROM THE 19TH TO 21ST CENTURIES

Much has changed on the Memphis landscape since it was founded on May 22, 1819, yet the city has enjoyed one interesting consistency: an active tourist trade. Davy Crockett was one of Memphis' most frequent visitors in the early days. He enjoyed many a rowdy time with friends like Sam Houston and Andrew Jackson at the infamous Bell Tavern. It was from the Memphis bluffs in the early 1840s that Davy said goodbye to his Tennessee friends for the last time as he crossed the Mississippi on his fateful journey to the Alamo.

Early settlers liked to stay here on their way out west, and others stopped by as they traveled north and south along the largest river in North America, the Mississippi. River workers, farmers, field laborers, and Delta high society all paid regular visits to the "City of Good Abode," as it was known, for

both its high culture and its "less-refined" diversions as well.

The Civil War period hosted thousands of armed visitors from the north, who, despite their less than cordial welcome, remained for several years, leaving behind a lot of their much-needed cash. The Federals occupied Memphis during most of the war (from 1863 on, to be exact), which is why so little of the city was destroyed.

Just as Memphis began to fully recover from the Civil War, it was devastated by the yellow fever epidemic of the 1870s and 1880s. The city's population was reduced by a third during this time, and Memphis lost its charter. However, the vision, determination, and civic pride on the part of Robert Church, the South's first black millionaire, provided the bonds needed for the city to regain both its charter and its place as a thriving Southern community.

In the 19th century and first half of the 20th century, regional tourists as well as a fair share of national and international tourists were drawn to Memphis. Many visitors came here for concerts, balls, family reunions, lectures, and the Orpheum's vaudeville shows.

Employment opportunities, major commerce, and entertainment lured African-Americans to a legendary street called Beale, where W.C. Handy and his great legacy, the blues, first found fame.

Today, Memphis is the largest city in the state. Instead of dirt paths and Native-American trade routes, Memphis is surrounded by a massive interstate system. Many of Memphis and Shelby County's most popular and successful new attractions have been developed just within the past 25 years. (Tourism got its biggest boost in 1982, the year Graceland opened to the public.) Now Memphis and Shelby County attract an estimated eight million tourists a year — many times over the city's 1820 resident population of 364.

Categorically Memphis

Free Stuff
Good for all ages.

Art Museum of the University of Memphis - Free daily
Fire Museum of Memphis - Free Tuesdays: 3-5 p.m.
Libertyland – Kids three and under, adults 55 and over always free

MEMPHIS PINK PALACE MUSEUM

∞ Memphis Tidbit
By 1835, the city's population had grown to more than 1,000 residents, and Memphis purchased its very first train. Only minutes after the locomotive's arrival did residents and community leaders realize no one in town knew how to drive it!

THE PEABODY DUCKS

Memphis Pink Palace Museum
Free Tuesdays: 1-4 p.m.
Memphis Brooks Museum of Art
Free Wednesdays: all day
Memphis Zoo – Free Tuesdays: 2-5 p.m.
Mud Island River Park – Free daily if you walk the bridge (does not include museum). Kids four and under always free.
National Civil Rights Museum – Free Mondays: 3-5 p.m., kids four and under always free.
National Ornamental Metal Museum – Kids five and under always free.
Peabody Ducks – Free daily (ducks march at 11 a.m. & 5 p.m.)

Memphis Music
All ages welcome but best for ages 10 and older.

Beale Street Historic District
Graceland
Sun Studio
Center for Southern Folklore
W.C. Handy House Museum
Gibson Guitar Factory
Memphis Rock'n'Soul Museum
Stax Museum of American Soul Music

Clubs, Shopping
Family friendly until around 9 p.m., then — get a babysitter.

Beale Street Historic District
The Pinch District
Overton Square
Cooper-Young District
South Main Street Arts District
Peabody Place Entertainment and Retail Center
Southland Greyhound Park (West Memphis, AR)
The Casinos of Tunica, MS

Historic Destinations
Family friendly, and the kids might actually learn something.

Davies Manor Plantation
Victorian Village
Magevney House

Memphis Queen Line
Mississippi River Museum
The Peabody Hotel
Elmwood Cemetery
A. Schwab's Dry Goods Store
Mud Island River Park
Police Museum
Main Street Trolley

Black History
Great for the whole family.

Mason Temple
National Civil Rights Museum
Slavehaven/Burkle Estate Museum

Pure Family Fun
All ages welcome.

The Children's Museum
    of Memphis
Fire Museum of Memphis
Memphis Zoo
Lichterman Nature Center
Memphis Pink Palace
    Museum & Planetarium
Union Planters Imax Theater
Libertyland Amusement Park
The Peabody Ducks
Laser Quest
Putt-Putt Family Park

The Sporting Life
For kids of all ages.

Memphis Redbirds at AutoZone
    Park (AAA Baseball)
The Memphis Grizzlies at
    FedExForum (NBA Basketball)
Memphis RiverKings (Hockey)
Memphis Motorsports Park
    (NASCAR & NHRA)
University of Memphis Tiger
    Basketball
University of Memphis Tiger
    Football
Olympic Baseball at the USA
    Baseball Stadium

Visual & Performing Arts
All ages.

Memphis Brooks Museum of Art
Dixon Gallery & Gardens
Memphis Botanic Garden
Art Museum at the University
    of Memphis
National Ornamental Metal
    Museum
Wonders: The Memphis
    International Cultural Series
Peabody Place Museum
South Main Street Arts District
Bartlett Community Theatre
Bartlett Performing Arts Center
Blues City Cultural Center
Ewing Children's Theatre
Morgan Woods Theatre
Harrell Performing Arts Theatre
Buckman Performing Arts Center
Germantown Community Theatre
Germantown Performing
    Arts Centre
Germantown Symphony Orchestra
Theatre Memphis
Orpheum Theatre
Playhouse on the Square
Circuit Playhouse
TheatreWorks
Opera Memphis
Memphis Symphony Orchestra
Iris: The Orchestra
Ballet Memphis
Classical Ballet Memphis
Cannon Center for the
    Performing Arts

THE MEMPHIS GRIZZLIES

THIRD-LARGEST RAIL CENTER

In a League of Their Own
Age appropriateness varies.

Belle Aire Biplane Rides
Biblical Resource Center
   and Museum
Cordova Cellars Winery
   & Vineyards
Danny Thomas/ALSAC Pavilion
Viking Culinary Arts Center

Busy Hands
All ages .

Clayworks
Paint-A-Piece Pottery
Saturday School at Memphis
   College of Art
Seize the Clay

Memphis Fun Facts & Trivia
(Test Optional)

Memphis is a lot of things to a lot of
people. Most notably, the city is...
...Named for its Egyptian sister city
on the Nile.
...Known as "The City of Trees," "The

LARGEST SPOT COTTON-TRADING
MARKET IN THE WORLD

City of Good Abode," "The Bluff City,"
and "America's Distribution Center."
...The largest city in Tennessee and
18th largest in the nation.
...Ranked by the Travel Industry
Association as one of the top 20
destinations for people traveling to
see or participate in a sporting event.
...The Pork BBQ Capital of the World,
producer of the largest BBQ cook-off in
the world (every May), and home to more
than 100 BBQ specialty restaurants.
...The home of historic Beale Street,
voted America's second most popular
entertainment district (behind

Bourbon Street).
...Home of the Pyramid, "Tomb of
Doom," the third largest pyramid in
the world.
...Ranked 6th in the nation in the
number of properties on the National
Register of Historic Places — with
more listings per capita than any city
in America.
...The largest spot cotton-trading
market in the world.
...The hardwood lumber capital of the
world.
...Home to the world's largest cargo
airport.
...The 3rd-largest rail center in the U.S.
...The 4th-largest inland port in the U.S.
Headquarters for:
AutoZone, Back Yard Burger, FedEx,
International Paper, Morgan-Keegan,
Orgill Brothers, Sharp Manufacturing,
Storage U.S.A., Buckman Laboratories,
Ducks Unlimited, Elvis Presley
Enterprises, and dozens of other
major companies.
...Home to St. Jude Children's
Research Hospital, founded by actor
Danny Thomas.

More about Memphis Music

Memphis is known worldwide for its music, and visitors want to see not only how legends were made, but how they lived. As a result, Graceland is the world's most famous music mecca. Presley's home is at once a monument to success and the trappings of fame.

One fateful day in 1954, Elvis sauntered into Sam Phillips' Memphis Recording Service (now called Sun Studio), and history was made. Roy Orbison, Johnny Cash, Jerry Lee Lewis, Ike Turner, and B.B. King are just some of the folks who launched their careers in Memphis, and you can still hear their outtakes during a Sun Studio tour.

The region's musical and cultural history are also preserved and promoted at the Memphis Rock'n'Soul Museum, developed by the Smithsonian Institution. This one-of-a-kind experience presents not just music milestones, but also a vivid portrait of the people, culture, circumstances, and the historic context that led to the evolution of the area's music.

And where would the modern western world be without "Soul Man" and "Sittin' on the Dock of the Bay"? It was Memphis of the 1960s and 1970s, where Soul Music was born. It was a raw and rhythmic reaction to the era of civil rights and free love. Proud of its past and eager to preserve it, the new Stax Museum of American Soul Music recreates the studio's heyday with tributes to Booker T. & the MGs, Otis Redding, Carla & Rufus Thomas, and many others, including the Rev. Al Green, who still occasionally leads his congregation in Sunday services at Memphis' Full Gospel Tabernacle Church.

Milestones in Memphis Music
(& Tidbits of American Trivia)

1912
W.C. Handy publishes "The Memphis Blues"
1936
The Overton Park Orchestra Shell is constructed by the WPA and the City of Memphis
1948
WDIA, America's first all-black radio station, goes on the air in Memphis
1949
Red Hot & Blue with host Dewey Phillips debuts on WHBQ radio
1950
Memphis Recording Service (aka Sun Studio) founded by Sam Phillips at 706 Union
1951
"Rocket 88" recorded by Jackie Brenston at Sun Studio and later becomes a #1 single
1952
Sun Records label created by Sam Phillips
1952
"3 O'Clock Blues" by B.B. King spends five weeks at #1 on the R&B chart
1953
Sun - "Bear Cat" by Rufus Thomas - #3 R&B
6/1/53
Elvis Presley pays four dollars at Sun Studio for a custom session

SUN STUDIO

1953
Sun - "Mystery Train" by Little Junior Parker - #5 R&B
7/5/54
Elvis Presley records "That's Alright" and "Blue Moon of Kentucky" at Sun Studio
7/30/54
Elvis Presley plays his first paid show, opening for Slim Whitman at the Overton Park Shell
1955
Sun - "Mystery Train" by Elvis Presley - #1 Country

1955
WHER, America's first all-female radio station, goes on the air in Memphis.
1956
Sun - "Folsom Prison Blues" by Johnny Cash - #5 Country
1956
Sun - "I Walk the Line" by Johnny Cash - #2 Country
1956
Sun -"Blue Suede Shoes" by Carl Perkins - #1 Country and R&B charts

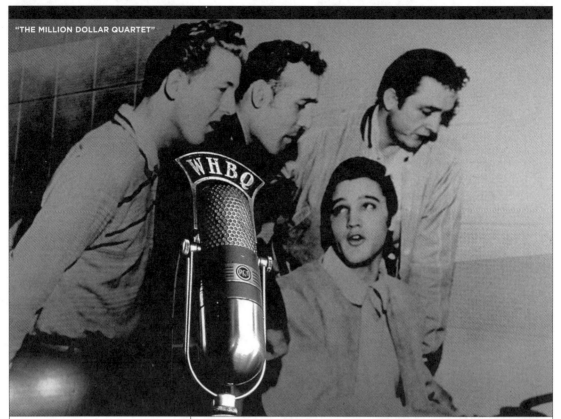

"THE MILLION DOLLAR QUARTET"

STAX RECORDS

12/4/56
"The Million Dollar Quartet" -
Johnny Cash, Jerry Lee Lewis,
Carl Perkins and Elvis Presley -
record at Sun Studio

1957
Elvis Presley appears on the *Ed Sullivan*
Show, but only from the waist up.

1957
Sun - "Whole Lotta Shakin'
Going On" by Jerry Lee Lewis -
#3 Pop and #1 Country and R&B

1957
Sun - "Great Balls of Fire" by
Jerry Lee Lewis - #2 Pop and #1
Country and R&B

1958
Sun - "Breathless" by Jerry Lee Lewis
- Top 10 Pop and Country charts

1959
"Memphis, Tennessee" by Chuck
Berry is released

1960
Stax Records opens at 926 E.
McLemore

1960
Stax - "Gee Whiz" by Carla Thomas
- Top 10 Pop and R&B charts

1961
Stax - "Last Night" by the Mar-
Keys - Top 5 Pop and R&B charts

1962
Stax - "Green Onions" by Booker
T. & the MG's - #1 R&B
The audio-cassette is invented.

1962
Stax - "I'll Bring It Home to

You" by Carla Thomas - #9 R&B

1963
Stax - "Walking the Dog" by
Rufus Thomas - Top 10 Pop and
R&B charts

1965
Stax - "Mr. Pitiful" by Otis
Redding - #10 R&B

1965
Stax - "I've Been Loving You Too Long (To Stop Now)" by Otis Redding - #2 R&B
1965
"Wooly Bully" by Sam the Sham & the Pharaohs - #2 Pop
1965
"Keep On Dancing" by the Gentrys - #4 Pop
1965
Stax - "You Don't Know Like I Know" by Sam and Dave - #7 R&B
1966
Stax - "Hold On! I'm Coming" by Sam and Dave - #1 R&B
1966
Stax - "Knock on Wood" by Eddie Floyd - #1 R&B
1966
Stax - "Try a Little Tenderness" by Otis Redding - #4 R&B
1967
Stax - "When Something is Wrong With My Baby" - #2 R&B
1967
Stax - "Soulfinger" by the Bar-Kays - #3 R&B
1967
"Born Under a Bad Sign" by Albert King is released on Stax Records
1967
Stax - "Soul Man" by Sam and Dave - #1 R&B and #2 Pop
1967
"The Letter" by the Box Tops - #1 Pop
1968
Stax - "I Thank You" by Sam and Dave — Top 10 Pop and R&B charts
1968
"Cry Like a Baby" by the Box Tops - #2 Pop
1968
Stax - "Sittin' on the Dock of the Bay" by Otis Redding - #1 Pop and R&B
1968
Stax - "Hang 'Em High" by Booker T. & the MG's - #9 Pop
1969
"Son of a Preacher Man" by Dusty Springfield (recorded in Memphis) - #5 Pop
1969
"Hot Buttered Soul" by Isaac Hayes becomes the first gold album on Stax Records
1969
"Suspicious Minds" by Elvis Presley - #1 Pop
1969
"In the Ghetto" by Elvis Presley - #3 Pop
1969
"Sweet Caroline" by Neil Diamond (recorded in Memphis) - #4 Pop
1970
"The Thrill is Gone" by B.B. King
1970
Stax - "Do the Funky Chicken" by Rufus Thomas - #5 R&B
1970
Hi - "Tired of Being Alone" by Al Green - #7 R&B
1970
Stax - "Do the Push and Pull

AL GREEN

(Part 1)" by Rufus Thomas - #1
R&B
1970
Led Zeppelin records portions of
III at Ardent Studios
1971
The soundtrack from *Shaft* is
released on Stax, hits #1 on both
the Pop and R&B charts
1972
Stax - "Never Can Say Goodbye"
by Isaac Hayes - #5 R&B
1972
Stax - "Respect Yourself" by the
Staples Singers - #2 R&B

1972
Stax - "I'll Take You There" by
the Staples Singers - #1 Pop & R&B
1972
Hi - "Let's Stay Together" by Al
Green - #1 Pop & R&B
1972
#1 Record by Big Star
1972
Stax - "(If Loving You is Wrong)
I Don't Want to Be Right" by
Luther Ingram - #1 R&B
1972
Hi - "I'm Still in Love With You"
by Al Green - Top 3 Pop and R&B

1972
Hi - "Look What You've Done
for Me" by Al Green - Top 5 Pop
and R&B
1972
Hi - "You Ought to Be with Me"
by Al Green - Top 3 Pop and R&B
7/21/73
Elvis Presley records at Stax studios
1973
Hi - "Here I Am (Come and Take
Me)" by Al Green - Top 10 Pop
& R&B
1973
ZZ Top records *Tres Hombres* at
Ardent Studios
1974
Hi - "Sha-La-La (Make Me
Happy)" by Al Green - Top 10
Pop & R&B
1974
Hi - "I Can't Stand the Rain" by
Ann Peebles - #6 R&B
1975
Furry Lewis opens for the Rolling
Stones at Liberty Bowl Memorial
Stadium
1975
Hi - "Take Me to the River" by
Syl Johnson - #7 R&B
1975
Hi - "L-O-V-E" by Al Green -
#1 R&B
1976
Al Green opens the Full Gospel
Tabernacle Church
1976
"Disco Duck" by Rick Dees - #1 Pop
1977
The U.S. Congress officially des-
ignates Memphis "The Home of
the Blues"
1980
The Blues Foundation founded
in Memphis
1980
First annual W.C. Handy Blues
Awards
1985
"Class of '55" sessions at Sun
Studio feature Johnny Cash,
Jerry Lee Lewis, Roy Orbison,
and Carl Perkins
1985
Kallen Esperian wins Pavarotti
International Voice Competition

ELVIS PRESLEY

RUFUS THOMAS

1996
Weekly *Beale Street Caravan* radio program debuts on National Public Radio

1996
Memphian Justin Timberlake joins N'Sync

2000
Shake Hands with Shorty by the North Mississippi Allstars nominated for Grammy award

2000
When the Smoke Clears by the Three 6 Mafia - #4 album

2000
Memphis rockers Saliva sign with Island Records

2001
Saliva's major-label debut *Every Six Seconds* goes gold

2003
Justin Timberlake greets the nation from Beale Street during "Dick Clark's New Year's Rockin' Eve" television broadcast

2003
Timberlake's solo album *Justified* released and later earns the singer five Grammy nominations. He wins two, including best Pop Album of the Year.

2003
Two Memphis bands, Saliva and the Porch Ghouls, open national tour for KISS and Aerosmith

2004
Memphis celebrates 50 years of rock'n'roll on July 5th — the date Elvis recorded "That's Alright" at Sun

2005
Jerry Lee Lewis performs "Whole Lotta Shakin' Goin' On" at the Rock and Roll Hall of Fame induction ceremony

and becomes a world-renowned soprano.

1987
U2 records songs on their *Rattle and Hum* album at Sun Studio

1989
R.E.M. releases *Green*, recorded at Ardent Studios

1989
Stevie Ray Vaughan records *In Step* at Kiva Studios

1991
"Walking in Memphis" leads Marc Cohn to a Grammy award as "Best New Artist"

1991
Memphian Cordell Jackson duels Brian Setzer in memorable Budweiser commercial

1991
The first Crossroads Music Exposition & Showcase is held

1993
"Come in Out of the Rain" by Wendy Moten

1994
The Grifters' *Crappin' You Negative* receives 4-star review in *Rolling Stone*

1994
"Talkin' Seáttle Grunge Rock Blues" by Todd Snider

1994
Gotta Feelin' by O'Landa Draper & the Associates debuts at #1 on the Gospel chart

1995
Sonic Youth records *Washing Machine* at Easley Studio

Notable Memphians

Actresses Kathy Bates, Cybill Shepherd, Dixie Carter, and cowgirl Dale Evans **Actors** Morgan Freeman, the late Michael Jeter, and George Hamilton **Baseball star** Tim McCarver and **Radio Jock** Rick Dees **Writers** Peter Taylor, Shelby Foote, and Tennessee Williams, writer/adventurer Richard Halliburton **Photographers** Bill Eggleston and Ernest Withers **Artists** Carroll Cloar and Burton Callicott **Fashion Designers** Dana Buchman, Pat Kerr, and Hilton McConnico

MEMPHIS & SHELBY COUNTY STATISTICS

Founded: 1819
Incorporated: 1826
Population in 1820: 364
1900: 102,320
1994: 614,289
Current Metropolitan Area: 1,400,151
Average Annual Temperature: 61.9 F (16.61 C)
Summer Average: 81.2 F (27.33 C)
Winter Average: 41.2 F (5.11 C)
Rainfall Average: 48.6 inches
Snowfall Average: 5.3 inches
Relative Humidity: 69%
Government: Mayor/City Council (est. 1966)
Average Elevation: 331 feet
Area: 18th largest city in the U.S. with 295.5 square miles
Tax: sales 9.25%, hotel 13.25%
Shelby County
Established: 1819
Population in 1996: 867,409
Government: Mayor/Board of Commissioners (est. 1974)
Area: 772 square miles
Memphis is in the Central Standard Time Zone.

Memphis International Airport

One of the nation's busiest airports, the Memphis International Airport is, in fact, the largest cargo airport in the world. It also serves as a major hub for Northwest Airlines. Four other major carriers and five regional carriers offer more than 500 flights per day. KLM Royal Dutch Airlines provides regular, direct flights to Amsterdam with

MEMPHIS INTERSTATE SYSTEM

connections to 149 cities in 83 countries. The Memphis International Airport is 15 minutes from downtown.

Major Interstates

Memphis sits on the borders of Tennessee, Arkansas, and Mississippi. As in most large cities, you should try to avoid rush hour. You will especially want to keep a safe distance if it rains, sleets, or snows. Memphians don't cope well with precipitation.

It's pretty easy to get around Memphis. Most of the city is laid out in a north-south grid. With a few exceptions, avenues run east and west. Downtown overlooks the river with the city spreading towards the east from there.

*Interstate 55 runs through Arkansas to the west of town, then heads south, connecting Memphis to Mississippi.
*Interstate 40 runs on the north before heading east to Nashville.
*Interstate 240 loops around the south and east. It also divides downtown from Midtown, connecting I-40 and I-55.

ALL AREA CODES are 901 unless noted.

Traveling by Rail and River

AMTRAK
800-USA-RAIL
Trains run daily through Memphis' Central Station, downtown. The rail system is a direct link between Memphis–New Orleans and Memphis–Chicago, a route often called America's Blues Highway.

Riverbarge Excursion Lines
(Based in New Orleans)
504-365-0022
888-GO BARGE, 462-2743
www.riverbarge.com
The 198-guest *River Explorer* hosts four-to-10-day cruises along America's inner waterways, stopping at major ports including New Orleans, St. Louis, Memphis, and others.

Delta Queen Steamboat Company
(Based in New Orleans)
800-543-1949
www.deltaqueen.com
The country's oldest Mississippi River cruise line invites you to dis-

cover Mark Twain's 19th-century America aboard an authentic paddlewheel steamboat.

Local Sightseeing and Touring Companies

American Dream Safari
527-8870
www.americandreamsafari.com
From the back roads of the Delta to the neon lights of a downtown Saturday night, take a cultural expedition inside a 1955 Cadillac.

Belle Air Biplane Rides
481-1935
www.belleaireaviation.com
Aerial sightseeing of Memphis and the Mississippi River aboard a 1930s-style biplane.

Blues City Tours
522-9229
www.memphisite.com/bluescity
Daily tours of Memphis and attractions plus casino and airport shuttles.

Carriage Tours of Memphis
527-7542
www.carriagetoursofmemphis.com
Enjoy the charm of a horse-drawn tour through historic downtown Memphis.

Destination King
766-1836
www.destinationking.com

Customized group tours and events.

Coach USA Memphis
382-6366, 800-222-0089
www.coachusa.us
Daily sightseeing, multi-lingual step-on guides, group tours, and charter service.

Heritage Tours
527-3427
www.heritagetoursmemphis.com
Cultural and historical tours of Memphis highlighting African-American sights and contributions plus all local attractions. Also visits Alex Haley House Museum in Henning, TN.

Memphis Queen Line Riverboats
527-5694, 800-221-6197
www.memphisqueen.com
Cruise the mighty Mississippi River with sightseeing trips by day and dinner & entertainment cruises by night.

Ride the Ducks of Memphis
521-DUCK
www.memphisducks.com
Take an entertaining, amphibious tour — with free Wacky Quackers.
Seasonal: April 1 - November 30.

Shangri-La Projects Ultimate Rock 'n' Roll Tours
359-3102
www.memphisrocktour.com

From Sherman Willmott, creator of *Kreature Comforts Low-Life Guide to Memphis* and founder of Shangri-La Records. Customized music-themed tours and pilgrimages for discerning fans.

Unique Tours
526-7777, 800-235-1984
www.uniquememphis.com
Specializing in hotel and attraction vacation packages and tours for individuals and groups.

Wolf River Conservancy – Canoe Trips
452-6500
Group trips on area rivers, including the Wolf River.

Wolf River Canoe Trips and Rentals
(Moscow, TN)
877-3958
Groups are invited to canoe down the scenic Wolf River.

Kayak Tours c/o Outdoors, Inc.
458-9925
Sunset cruises on the Mississippi. Few experiences can compare.

TRAVEL AGENCIES

A & I Travel Service, Inc.
291-1400
www.aitvl.com

Great American Cruises, Inc.
525-5302
www.greatamericancruises.com

Omega World Travel
821-9442
www.owt.net

Sekisui International
273-0123

Travelennium, Inc.
767-0761, 800-844-4924
www.travelennium.com

Unique Tours
526-7777, 800-235-1984
www.uniquememphis.com

MEMPHIS QUEEN LINE RIVERBOATS

Public Transportation

Memphis is not famous for its public transportation. The majority of residents and visitors use private cars, and there is no subway system. However, the city does have an efficient bus system for mass transit (which includes operation of the Main Street Trolley Line), known locally as MATA. The popular Downtown Airport Shuttle (DASH) is also managed by MATA.

Of course, there are taxis and limo services, but this is the city's weakest link. I can personally vouch for Yellow Cab and Checker Cab. And for private cars or limos, I have had very good experiences working with Premier Transportation.

MATA
(Memphis Area Transit Authority)
274-6282
www.matatransit.com
City Bus Lines
274-6282
Main St. Trolley
274-6282
DASH
(Downtown Airport Shuttle)
522-1677

Cabs
Checker Cab
577-7777
City Wide Cab Company
324-4202, 722-8294
Yellow Cab
577-7777
Downtown Buggy
(3-wheel "pedi-cabs")
529-9677

Limousines and Private Transportation
Everything Xpress
454-7223
Premier Transportation
577-7777
www.premierofmemphis.com
Tennessee Limousine Service
452-6207, 800-207-9499
www.tennesseelimo.com
The Memphis Bar Hopper
(attraction shuttle)
362-5331

The Bette Bus
360-8747
Transportation to/from Memphis and the Little Rock Airport

Car Rentals
Avis Rent-A-Car
2520 Rental Road
345-2847, 800-331-1212
2 locations
www.avis.com
Budget Car and Truck Rental
398-8888, 800-879-1227
4 locations
Enterprise Rent-A-Car
380-7700, 800-RENT-A-CAR
15 locations
www.enterprise.com
National Car Rental
2680 Rental Road
345-0070
www.nationalcar.com

Outdoor Recreation Information

Water Sports
Memphis Yacht Club
525-3808
Riverside Park Marina
946-2000
Sam's Jet Ski & Boat Rental
486-2470
681-6581 (pager)

Fishing & Hunting
Tennessee Wildlife Resources Agency
800-372-3928

State Parks
T.O. Fuller State Recreational Park
543-7581
Meeman Shelby State Park
876-5215
Shelby Farms
382-0235
www.shelbycountytn.gov

On the Links
Cherokee Valley Golf Club
525-GOLF
www.olivebranchgolf.com/cherokee.asp
Glen Eagle Golf Course
874-5168
www.nsamidsouth.navy.mil

Kirkwood National Golf Club
800-461-4653, 662-252-4888
Memphis National Golf Club
853-8058
www.palmergolf.com
Memphis Park Commission Courses
454-5200
www.cityofmemphis.org
Plantation Golf Club
525-2411, 662-895-3530
www.olivebranchgolf.com
Shelby County Edmund Orgill Park
872-7493
Stonebridge Golf Course
382-1886
www.stonebridgegolf.com
T.O. Fuller State Park
543-7771

Visitor Information
543-5333
www.memphistravel.com
Two Shelby County visitor center locations:
Memphis/Shelby County Visitors Center
12036 Arlington Trail
Memphis Visitors Center
3205 Elvis Presley Boulevard

CHAPTER 2

Downtown

Take me to the river

HERNANDO DESOTO BRIDGE

DOWNTOWN MEMPHIS is arguably the most exciting and interesting part of the city. I have both lived and worked Downtown, so I can attest it's where the action is! In the past few years the area has experienced a real renaissance, enjoying the fruits of a few visionaries in the form of a shopping center, a new arena, old and new hotels, and, of course, bustling Beale Street.

As a general rule, most of the area's attractions are located between North Parkway and G.E. Patterson. Exceptions are Slavehaven on North Second Street (several blocks north of Poplar) and the Stax Museum of American Soul Music, which is in an area

south of Linden. Join the throngs who explore all over Memphis and enjoy every part of it.

Where It All Begins

Memphis was born because of the Mississippi River. The city is often referred to as the "Bluff City," because it sits atop tall bluffs, mounds of eroded mud that took millions of years to create. The river was — and is — its lifeblood. In the 1800s, the river also became the dividing line between Tennessee on the east side and Arkansas on the west. Then the state of Mississippi drew its line just south of the city. To make a long story short, Memphis began down-

town and grew from west to east.

Today, Memphis is divided into five general areas: Downtown, Midtown, East Memphis, North Memphis, and South Memphis (which includes the Airport Area). But the heart of the city, its pulse and essence, is Downtown. This is the area that has witnessed all the history, the tragedy and glory, the ruin of urban decay and the pride of its resurrection and ultimate renaissance.

Downtown Memphis is marked by glass highrises and 19th-century warehouses, haute cuisine restaurants and funky alley hideaways, art galleries and gift shops, plus live entertainment that literally rocks all night long. It's where the city's workforce blends with pioneer residents who, in turn, rub elbows with tourists from all over the world. It has an energy and an attitude all its own.

Downtown is also convenient. There are many hotels to choose from (several with heated pools), and more than half of the city's most popular attractions are within walking distance of each other or easily accessible by trolley.

Sites & Attractions

SCHWAB'S

A. Schwab's Dry Goods Store
163 Beale Street
523-9782
Monday-Saturday, 10 a.m.-5 p.m.

This three-story dry goods store is a Memphis landmark. Now in the hands of a fourth generation of Schwab family members, Schwab's is a charming, "old-timey" store that literally has it all: clothing, candy, voodoo potions, cooking utensils like huge cast-iron skillets, underwear, and souvenirs. You'll find 99-cent neckties and the world's largest overalls. There is also a modest Beale Street museum on the second level.

Many schools in the area bring children here on field trips. It's like going back in time. The store has operated virtually unchanged since its doors opened in 1876. (I've often thought that even the dust found on items tucked in the corners goes back more than 100 years.) I love this place. Kids can roam around for a *long* time, and the merchandise is very affordable.

AUTOZONE PARK

AutoZone Park/Memphis Redbirds
8 South Third Street
721-6050
www.memphisredbirds.com
Tours: 10 a.m. and 1 p.m. on non-game days
Length: 45 minutes-1 hour; guides available
Price: $4 for adults, $3 for seniors, military & children ages 1-14

This award-winning, state-of-the-art baseball park is the home of the Memphis Redbirds, the AAA farm team of the St. Louis Cardinals. (Interesting fact: The Redbirds and AutoZone Park are America's only not-for-profit baseball team and facility.) It's been called the finest ever built below the major leagues, and it's true, there are no bad seats.

Even if your kids don't want to sit through nine innings, they'll find plenty else to do. There's the Boardwalk, a carnival and arcade-like area that includes a batting cage, pitch speed indicator, and water gun race. There's also a 24-foot climbing wall and the Rocky Hopper amusement park-style ride, among other things. For the youngest tykes, there's P.D.

Parrot's Playhouse Perch with observation towers, a miniature baseball diamond, and other diversions to keep kids busy while parents enjoy the game.

In addition to its private skyboxes and the usual tiered seating, AutoZone Park features an open field behind third base, the Bluff, where fans can watch the game while children run free. On the east side of the field is the Picnic Pavilion—where there are enough picnic tables to accommodate 500 fans with field-level seating.

Tours are available during the off-season, too. You can peek behind the scenes to see the press box and the players' workout areas.

COMING SOON: The National Pastime Museum: A Celebration of Baseball in American Life. Working with the National Baseball Hall of Fame and the Smithsonian Institution — and officially sanctioned as the official museum of minor-league baseball — this new attraction will be adjacent to the ballpark. It will present a view of American history and culture against the backdrop of America's favorite pastime, following baseball from the Civil War into the 21st century.

Beale Street Entertainment District
Beale Street between South Main Street and Fourth Avenue
www.bealestreet.com

One of America's most famous streets is where you'll find more than 30 nightclubs, restaurants, and retail shops. Just take a stroll. Your daytime tour will be entirely different from a visit in the evening.

During the day, families enjoy souvenir "gathering" at the numerous little shops along the street. Several clubs and restaurants like B.B. King's and the Hard Rock Café also have gift shops. There is an official Beale Street Visitors Center that sells keepsakes, and Schwab's (see separate listing) is a real treat.

The Police Museum (inside the police station) is small but interesting. You can have your picture taken inside a cell and learn about some of the area's infamous residents, most notably Machine Gun Kelly. On the other end of this four-block entertainment district, you'll find the W.C. Handy House Museum. The home was moved to this location from elsewhere on Beale, but it still contains original family furnishings.

By night, Beale Street offers a nightlife that is hard to beat. Children are welcome to accompany their parents for dinner and to hear some of the evening's entertainment, but most clubs prefer that kids leave by 9 p.m. or so. You might have more fun on your own, too. (For babysitter information, see Chapter Eight.) Beale Street, especially on weekends and during the summer, parties all night. Alcohol is served until 5 a.m., and the musicians are truly some of the finest in the world. World-famous clubs and smaller "hidden treasures" abound.

Belle Aire Tours/Biplane Rides
See Millington section (Chapter Six) for details

Center for Southern Folklore & Café
119 South Main
525-3655
www.southernfolklore.com
Monday-Friday: 11 a.m.-5 p.m.
Saturday: Noon-6 p.m.
Donations welcome
Tour length: 1-3 hours, depending on interest

This is a family-friendly and smoke-free environment. Founded nearly 30 years ago by two documentary filmmakers who wanted to preserve Southern arts and crafts before they disappeared, this nonprofit center offers a wonderful insight into all things below the Mason-Dixon line with a heavy emphasis on the Delta. Video-tapes and musical recordings capture authentic blues artists of the region, both famous and anonymous. Literature, art work, and crafts are for sale. And the Center provides unique, entertaining, and highly informative walking tours of the Beale Street area.

Located within the dining area of Pembroke Square, you and the family can grab some lunch, and, oftentimes, live entertainment is available too. FYI: The Center for Southern Folklore produces one of the region's most popular festivals each year: the Memphis Music & Heritage Festival (*see Annual Events listings*).

HISTORIC BEALE STREET

FEDEXFORUM

FedExForum

Between Third and Fourth
Streets, Lt. George W. Lee & Linden
888-HOOPS
www.FedExForum.com
www.nba.com/grizzlies
Call or go online for game schedule
Grizzlies ticket prices: The
Weekend Pack starts at $99, the
Power Pack (15 games plus a tee-
shirt) starts at $126. Many other
options available. Open year-round.

This state-of-the-art sports
arena, home to Memphis' NBA
Grizzlies, is striking in its architectural style and in its comfortable,
user-friendly amenities.

Promising plenty of legroom,
excellent sightlines, and superior
acoustics, FedExForum covers 13.8
acres and can seat up to 19,000
people (18,400 Grizzly fans). *Be
sure to ask about the IronKids Grizz
Kids Fan Club.*

A major addition to the downtown skyline, the arena includes a
Team Store (open year-round),

Sports Bar, Club Restaurant, Club
Lounge, an event-level restaurant,
and interactive displays and exhibits.

In addition to basketball,
FedExForum accommodates a variety
of concerts and special events. An
extra bonus is the "attraction within an
attraction": the Memphis Rock'n'Soul
Museum (see separate listing).

Fire Museum of Memphis

118 Adams Avenue
320-5650
www.firemuseum.com
Monday-Saturday: 9 a.m.-5 p.m.
Closed Sunday
Price: $5 for adults, $4 for ages 3-
12 and 60+, kids under 2 are free
Tour length: 1 hour

Established inside an authentic,
19th-century fire station, this is a
classic example of "edu-tainment."
The Fire Museum offers a collection
of artifacts, photographs, and stories
of Memphis' most dramatic fires. It
also features real fire engines that
kids love to crawl on, an animated

FIRE MUSEUM OF MEMPHIS

"talking" horse, and interactive
games that teach safety. One of the
most talked-about exhibits is the Fire
Room, which may be a bit too
intense for very young children. If
nothing else, you'll emerge from
this exhibit saying "it's hot!"

Gibson Guitar Factory Tours

145 Lt. George W. Lee Avenue
543-0800
www.gibsonshowcase.com
Monday-Saturday: 11 a.m., noon,
1 p.m., 2 p.m.
Sunday: 1 p.m., 2 p.m.
Price: $10 for ages 12 and up
only
Tour length: 30 minutes
Restaurant on-site.

Docents take you onto the factory floor and lead you past 16 work stations that represent every major stage of producing some of the world's finest guitars. This is where "Lucille" and the "Les Paul" are produced. Children under 12 are not allowed on this tour (nor would they particularly enjoy it), but most older kids should find it interesting. My son's favorite part was the gift shop at the end of the tour, but he and his friends *always* like the gift shops.

GIBSON GUITAR FACTORY

JILLIAN'S

Historic Elmwood Cemetery
824 S. Dudley Street
774-3212
www.elmwoodcemetery.org
Open daily from 8 a.m.-4:30 p.m.
Price: Free admittance;
tour charges vary
Driving tour: 1 hour
Walking tour: varies

Personally, I love cemeteries and always have. (My husband actually proposed to me in a cemetery, but that's another story.) This place is beautiful. It's in a somewhat neglected area, caught between downtown and Midtown, but it is perfectly safe during the day. After traveling over an old, narrow bridge, you enter an expanse with hundreds of trees and a "tombstone history" of the area. Winding carriage paths weave you in and out of sculpture artworks. A lovely Victorian cottage sits at the main entrance. Inside you'll find information and docents who will gladly answer your questions and help tailor a tour to fit your interests. With children in tow, you may prefer to keep it simple with a self-guided drive tour. Lots of famous people are buried here, so it could serve as great history lesson material if you're interested.

Some of Elmwood's famous "residents" include: Professor Herman Arnold, original orchestrator of the tune "Dixie"; Robert Church, the South's first black millionaire; Kit Dalton, outlaw in the James Gang; E.H. Little, head of the Colgate-Palmolive Co.; Virginia "Ginny" Bethel Moon, Confederate spy; Dorothea Henry Winston, daughter of Patrick Henry; 17 Civil War generals; and many others with fascinating, personal stories to tell.

Jillian's
150 Peabody Place
543-8800
www.jillians.com
Sunday-Wednesday: 11 a.m.-1 a.m.
Thursday-Saturday: 11 a.m.-2 a.m.

Combining dining and entertainment, this complex includes a video café, an Amazing Game Room upstairs (with 150 arcade-style games), billiards in the Nine Ball Lounge, Atlas Dance Club, and a lower-level bowling alley called the Hi Life Lanes. Will and his friends love the bowling alley and the arcade area. While fun, it can get crowded, and in the evenings, the place becomes more adult-oriented.

Magevney House
198 Adams Avenue
523-1484
www.memphismuseums.org
Friday & Saturday: Noon-4 p.m.*
Closed January & February
Price: Donations welcome
Tour length: 20 minutes
Call before you go. City budget cuts occasionally dictate hours of operation.

In an area known as Victorian Village, this house belonged to one of Memphis' first schoolteachers. Built in the 1830s, it is a modest, white clapboard cottage. It doesn't take long to tour, but it captures the feeling of what life was like for the area's early pioneers. You should combine this tour with a visit to the neighboring and stately Mallory-Neely House. (The Woodruff-Fontaine house is another notable home just up the street. See individual listing.)

Main Street Trolley

274-6282

www.matatransit.com

(See downtown map for trolley stops)

Monday-Thursday: 6 a.m.-midnight

Friday: 6 a.m.-1 a.m.

Saturday: 9:30 a.m.-1 a.m.

Sunday: 10 a.m.-6 p.m.

Exact fare required: 60 cents, 30 cents for seniors and disabled. Special lunchtime fare (11:30 a.m. – 1:30 p.m.) is 30 cents. All-day trolley card is $2.50, three-day trolley card is $6.

Go back in time to the 19th century aboard these authentic, fully restored trolley cars. The North-South Main Street route connects to the scenic, 2.5-mile Riverfront Loop, linking riders with many attractions, including the Pyramid and Pinch District, Beale Street, Peabody Place, Orpheum Theatre, and the National Civil Rights Museum.

A recent expansion invites trolley fans aboard the Medical Center Rail Extension, which connects Downtown and the Medical Center. Much of this route is not exactly "scenic," but it'll take you down Madison Avenue to Cleveland, where you'll find Midtown's landmark Stewart Brothers Hardware store.

Mallory-Neely House

652 Adams Avenue

(Victorian Village)

523-1484

www.memphismuseums.org

Tuesday-Saturday: 10 a.m.- 4 p.m.*

Sunday: 1 – 4 p.m.

Closed January & February

$5 for adults, $4 for seniors

$3.50 for kids under 12

Tour length: 40 minutes

Call before you go. City budget cuts occasionally dictate hours of operation.

Built in 1852 in a neighborhood known as Victorian Village, this Italianate mansion includes most of its original furnishings. I lean towards the romantic, so I am mesmerized by the detailed architecture, beautiful furniture and silver services, costumes, and family lore. Personally, I love touring historic homes — especially when they are accompanied by ghost stories as these in Victorian Village are. But some children (and pardon me, but this seems especially true of boys rather than girls) have a short attention span when it comes to this kind of thing. You know your kids; you be the judge.

Memphis Police Museum

(Inside Downtown Precinct)

159 Beale Street

525-9800

www.bealestreet.com

7 days a week: 7 a.m. - 2 a.m.

Free

Tour length: 30 minutes

Located inside an active police station, the tiny Memphis Police Museum offers a little bit of something for all ages. The children will like having their picture taken inside a jail cell, and some kids will be fascinated by the uniforms and small guns on display. Grownups will enjoy reading about some of Memphis' more notorious criminals such as Machine Gun Kelly and James Earl Ray.

Memphis Queen Line Riverboats
45 Riverside Drive
527-BOAT, 800-221-6197
www.memphisqueen.com
June–August: Two cruises daily
at 2:30 p.m. and 5 p.m.
10:30 a.m. cruise on Friday
& Saturday
**April & May, September
& October:** Weekdays at 2:30
p.m., 4:30 p.m. on Saturday
& Sunday
March & November:
2:30 Friday and Saturday
Cost for day cruises: $14.50 for
adults, $12.50 for seniors, stu-
dents, military, $10.50 for ages
4-17, free for 3 and under
Evening music cruises
**April & May, September &
October:** 7:30 p.m.
June–August: 8 p.m.
Cost for evening cruises: $39.95
for adults, $36.95 for seniors,
students, military, $29.95 for
children, free for 3 and under
Tour length
Sightseeing cruises: 1.5 hours
Dinner cruises: 2 hours

Discover Mark Twain's Mississippi aboard the city's only paddle
wheeler riverboats. It's slow and
relaxing, and the captain provides a
guided tour along the way. Dinner
cruises last longer and include live
entertainment. It's a pleasant and
relaxing alternative for days that
may be over-packed and action-
packed. We had a really good time
on a recent 4th of July dinner
cruise. After a tasty BBQ supper, we
stopped just offshore for a spectacular view of the fireworks display.
There are occasional longer trips
available, too, most notably the
annual trip to Helena, Arkansas,
for the King Biscuit Blues Festival.
The trip includes a brief stop at a
sandbar, where you are invited to
get off and explore before resuming
the trip down river.
NOTE: As of the printing of this
book, the Queen Line is having
some financial difficulties. I recommend that you call ahead to

double-check tour times and
prices and to make reservations. If
there is no answer at the Queen
Line (they do get busy), call the
Memphis & Shelby County Visitor
Center for information at 543-
5333 or 888-633-9099.

Memphis Rock'n'Soul Museum
Between Third and Fourth
Streets, Lt. George W. Lee & Linden
543-0800
www.memphisrocknsoul.org
Open daily 10 a.m.–6 p.m.
Price: $8.50 for adults, $7.50
for seniors, $5 for ages 5-17
Tour length: 1.5-2 hours

Developed by the Smithsonian
Institution (with its only permanent exhibit outside of
Washington, D.C.), the Memphis
Rock'n'Soul Museum is more
than a collection of music memorabilia and costumes. It examines
the people, the history, and the
cultures of the South that, in
turn, created the music the region
is famous for. All roads lead to
Memphis, and this museum fol-
lows the trip from the Delta to
Beale Street, from the 1930s to
the 1970s. This is a superb museum and well worth your while.

Mississippi River Museum
(Located at Mud Island River
Park, see below)
125 North Front Street
576-7230
www.mississippirivermuseum.org
April 9–May 27:
Tuesday–Sunday, 10 a.m–5 p.m.
May 28-September 5:
Open 7 days a week, 10 a.m.–8 p.m.
September 6–October 31:
Tuesday–Sunday, 10 a.m.–5 p.m.
Price: $8 for adults
$6 for seniors (aged 60+)
$5 for ages 5-12
Tour length: 1–2 hours
Restaurant on-site

You can drive your car to Mud
Island (across the Auction Street
Bridge), walk over the bridge, or
ride the monorail just like Tom
Cruise did in *The Firm*. Whatever

MEMPHIS ROCK'N'SOUL MUSEUM

∾ MEMPHIS TIDBIT
Look for the giant LP on top of
the sign. It spins at 33 RPMs! Be
prepared to explain to the kids
what a record is.

mode of transportation you use,
it's worth the trip to see this 18-
gallery museum that focuses on the
natural and cultural history of the
Lower Mississippi River Valley.
More than 5,000 artifacts cover

river transportation, the American Civil War, the music of the Delta, and much more. Kids love walking through the replica of the paddle wheeler, and they especially like being in the midst of the Civil War gunship battle, explosions and all. The tour winds up at a 4,000-gallon aquarium and then, of course, a gift shop!

Mud Island River Park
125 North Front Street
576-7241, 800-507-6507
www.mudisland.com
Summer: 10 a.m. – 8 p.m.
Spring (April & May) & Fall (September & October):
10 a.m. – 5 p.m.
Closed Mondays and closed in the winter (November – March)
River Park is free. (Admission to Mud Island River Museum, see separate listing)
Tour length: 1-3 hours
Restaurant on-site

NATIONAL CIVIL RIGHTS MUSEUM

MUD ISLAND RIVER PARK

This 52-acre educational and recreational facility is all about the mighty Mississippi. In addition to the river museum (described above), its best-known feature is the 5-block-long River Walk, which is a miniature of the entire river from start to finish, complete with Gulf of Mexico. Rentals are available for canoes, kayaks, airboats, pedal boats, and bicycles. You can also get a bite to eat at a couple of casual, concession-like areas. And during the summer, a concert series fills the Mud Island Amphitheater, which faces the downtown skyline.

National Civil Rights Museum
450 Mulberry Street
521-9699
www.civilrightsmuseum.org
Monday, Wednesday – Saturday:
9 a.m. – 5 p.m.
Sunday: 1 p.m. – 5 p.m.
Closed Tuesdays
Price: $10 for adults, $8 for students (with ID) and seniors (aged 55+), $6.50 for ages 4-17, under 3 free
June – August: Open until 6 p.m.
Tour length: 1.5 hours

This is one of the country's finest and most important museums. It should be a priority for all families. Follow the trials and triumphs of the Civil Rights Movement through interpretive exhibits and audio-visual displays. Emphasis is on events of the mid-to-late 20th century. The message is inspiring and the presentation is extremely well done.

Built at the Lorraine Motel where Dr. Marin Luther King, Jr. was assassinated, you'll actually see the room he stayed in and the balcony where he died. Then you'll cross the street to see the property from the assassin's perspective. You'll also learn about what has been accomplished in the Civil Rights Movement since King's death.

This is a must though best-suited for school-age children. Check out the child's audio tour. For a hook, tell 'em about the long list of celebrities that have visited here like Orlando Bloom and U2 frontman Bono!

National Ornamental Metal Museum
374 Metal Museum Drive
774-6380
www.metalmuseum.org
Tuesday – Saturday:
10 a.m. – 5 p.m.
Sunday: noon – 5 p.m.
Closed Monday
Closed December 25 – January 1
Price: $4 for adults
$3 for seniors, $2 for students
under 5 free
Tour length: 45 minutes

A travel writer from *U.S.A. Today* told me this was his favorite Memphis attraction. It's a little hard to find but just a few minutes from Main Street and well worth the trip as it sits atop a tall bluff and offers a wonderful view of the Mississippi River. Occupying several historic buildings, the primary facility houses rotating exhibits (all kinds of artworks, including sculptures and jewelry, etc.), the museum's permanent exhibits, and one of the city's best gift shops.

Recently celebrating its 25th anniversary, this is the only museum in the world dedicated solely to metalworks, and its significance is appreciated worldwide. Across the sculptured yard from the main building is the blacksmith shop. You can watch the artisans creating new works and repairing old ones — and some of them are huge. It's worth noting that museums from all over the country send important artifacts here for repair. The staff will mend something of yours, too, at the annual Repair Days Weekend and Auction every October.

Orpheum Theatre
203 South Main Street
525-7800
www.orpheum-memphis.com
Usually 8 p.m. with weekend matinees at 2 p.m.
Ticket prices vary

THE ORPHEUM

"Where Broadway Meets Beale." This beautifully restored movie palace, built in 1928, hosts touring Broadway productions year-round, as well as ballet, opera, concerts, and other events. Typical Broadway shows include musicals like *The Lion King*, *Cats*, *Les Miserables* and *The Full Monty*. You might want to check out what's on stage while you're in town. Oftentimes, these shows feature original cast members, and many of the productions are great for children. The Orpheum also offers a movie series, complete with a performance on the theater's huge, historic Wurlitzer, which rises from below the stage. You haven't experi-

enced a movie until you've seen *Gone with the Wind* or *The Wizard of Oz* on a giant — and I mean giant — screen.

Peabody Ducks
149 Union Avenue
(inside the Peabody Hotel)
529-4000, 800-PEABODY
www.peabodymemphis.com
Twice daily: 11 a.m. and 5 p.m.
Free

One of the wackiest attractions in town is the parade of the Peabody Ducks. Twice a day, every day, the Peabody Hotel's most famous residents ride the elevator to and from their rooftop penthouse to waddle across the red carpet (accompanied by a John Philip Sousa march) for their day job: swimming around the large, ornate fountain in the middle of the hotel's lobby. It's a tradition that goes back more than 50 years involving the hotel manager and his

hunting buddies, a little too much of their favorite beverage, and an afterthought with decoy ducks that became a claim-to-fame. Hundreds of tourists fill the lobby every day to watch this two-minute performance, so I suggest you get there early (by 15 to 30 minutes) to stake out a decent vantage point.

Peabody Place Entertainment & Retail Center
150 Peabody Place
(adjacent to the Peabody Hotel)
261-PLAY
www.belz.com
Open seven days a week - hours vary per business
Restaurants, shops, movies, and recreation

Conveniently attached to the Peabody Hotel, Peabody Place can keep the family entertained for hours. It includes several restaurants (Isaac Hayes' Music Food and Passion, Dan McGuinness Irish Pub, Texas de Brazil, Maggie Moo's, Starbucks) and shops (The Gap, Victoria's Secret, Tower Records, Ann Taylor Loft), plus the 21-screen Muvico Theatre, NASCAR simulated car-racing arcade, and glow-in-the-dark miniature golf. The Jillian's "complex" includes a video café, Hi-Life Bowling Lanes, Amazing Games

PEABODY PLACE

∾ MEMPHIS TIDBIT
The Muvico Theatre offers a babysitting service (ages 3-8) for up to three hours while parents attend the movies. Children are supervised by certified teachers, and parents are given pagers in case of an emergency. It costs $7 per child. Call 248-0101 for information and reservations.

arcade (with virtual bowling), Atlas Dance disco, and billiards.

Some places such as Starbucks open early. Most places are open late. Jillian's can get a bit rowdy after 9 p.m. on weekends, so you might want to keep a tight leash on young children if you want to roam around later in the evening.

Peabody Place Museum
119 South Main Street
523-ARTS
www.belz.com/museum/index.html
Tuesday – Friday:
10 a.m. – 5:30 p.m.
Saturday & Sunday:
noon – 5 p.m.
Closed Monday
Price: $5 for adults
$4.50 for seniors, $4 for students
Tour length: 1 hour

Tour one of the country's largest collections of historic Chinese art from the Qing (Ch'ing) Dynasty (1644-1911), including massive and mind-boggling jade sculptures, ivory carvings, and cloisonné. The museum also includes Judaica, Russian lacquer boxes, Italian mosaics, and other unique artifacts.

Generally speaking, this is best for school-aged kids and older, but most children are awed by the scale and detail of the jade works.

Putting Edge
150 Peabody Place
523-0204
www.puttingedge.com
Monday – Thursday:
11 a.m. – 10 p.m.
Friday & Saturday: 1 a.m. – 1 a.m.
Price: $6 for adults, $5 for children 6 and under - before 6 p.m.
After 6 p.m.: $7 for adults, $6 for 6 and under

We always have fun playing the occasional round of miniature golf, but we all got especially excited about the Putting Edge. It glows in the dark! It sort of feels like a 1960s meeting between Alice in Wonderland and the

Wizard of Oz; the place is filled with almost surreal, bright neon lights. I took several boys with me to test it out. My son Will summed it up succinctly as "awesome."

St. Jude Children's Research Hospital – Danny Thomas/ALSAC Pavilion
332 North Lauderdale
495-3306
www.stjude.org
Sunday – Friday: 8 a.m. – 4 p.m.
Saturday: 10 a.m. – 4 p.m.
Free admission
Tour length: 30-45 minutes

St. Jude offers free medical care to children from all over the world who suffer from cancer or similar life-threatening illness. Founded by the late entertainer Danny Thomas, the pavilion showcases a history of the hospital plus its various charities. It also offers a look at the comedian's career and serves as his final resting place.

Slavehaven Underground Railroad Museum — also known as the Burkle Estate
826 North Second Street
527-3427
www.heritagetoursmemphis.com
Summer
Monday – Saturday:
10 a.m. – 4 p.m.
Winter
Wednesday – Saturday:
10 a.m. – 4 p.m.
Price: $6 for adults, $4 for students
Tour length: 30-45 minutes
Call ahead to reserve a tour.

Reputed way-station on the Underground Railroad, this modest house features a cellar and trap doors used for escape by runaway slaves. Displays of artifacts help tell the story of slavery in Memphis.
FYI: Slavehaven is north of downtown's main tourist area, but it's close — only a few minutes' drive. You can pull up in front of the house and park right on the street.
NOTE: This is not a heavily trafficked area; so visit during the daytime.

STAX MUSEUM

Soulsville U.S.A.: Stax Museum of American Soul Music
926 East McLemore
946-2535
www.soulsvilleusa.com
March – October
Monday – Saturday: 9 a.m. – 5 p.m.
Sunday: 1 – 5 p.m.
November – February
Monday – Saturday: 10 a.m. – 5 p.m.
Sunday: 1 – 5 p.m.
Closed some holidays
Price: $9 for adults, $8 for ages 62+ and military, $6 for ages 9-12, under 8 free with adult
Tour length: 1.5 hours

Named for the neighborhood that produced so many of the city's most famous musicians and performers, the Stax Museum is Memphis' newest and one of its finest attractions. It does more than celebrate the great soul music of the 1960s and 1970s. It offers a look at the culture and music genres that led to the development of soul music as well as the artists worldwide who were influenced by this uniquely Memphis sound. Featured artists include Otis Redding, Aretha Franklin, Booker T. & the MG's, Isaac Hayes, and many others. It's a state-of-the-art facility that presents its subject with style and substance.

The museum's location is a bit out

Sun Studio

706 Union Avenue
521-0664
www.sunstudio.com
Open daily 10 a.m.-6 p.m.
Closed some holidays
Price: $9.50

Take a guided tour through the history of rock'n'roll. In fact, Sun Studio is credited with being the actual birthplace of rock'n'roll. The tour includes outtakes from sessions and a superb narrative by one of several knowledgeable guides. You can even touch Elvis' first microphone. You really feel like you've gone back in time and that you are on hallowed ground as you learn about the early careers of Elvis, Jerry Lee Lewis, B.B. King, Johnny Cash, Carl Perkins, and many other music pioneers. **FYI:** This tiny studio is still an active recording center for some of today's most famous recording stars. The kids may not be all that impressed that the studio is listed on the National Registry of Historic Places, but a lot of them will love the idea that they can make their own record here. For a fee, you can book the studio by the hour (after it closes to the sightseeing public) and cut your own "hit single" under the direction of a real recording engineer.

Victorian Village

198-680 Adams Avenue
www.memphismuseums.org

Grand historic homes (some privately owned and some open to the public) stand as testament to the lifestyles of some of Memphis' early families. In the mid-1800s, this area was on the outskirts of town. Now it's in the shadow of downtown. It's a pleasure simply to stroll the sidewalk amid the street's giant, ancient trees. Right across the street from the neighborhood's biggest attractions is Cielo, a unique restaurant, also housed in a Victorian mansion, that offers

SUN STUDIO

of the way, but it's only about five minutes from Beale Street, and it's well worth the trip. There's plenty of parking around back, with a security guard on-site.

South Main Street Arts District

South Main Street between
Beale and G.E. Patterson
www.southmainmemphis.org

This is *the* hot spot, an area that went from neglect and decay to renovation and resurrection. The South Main Street Arts District has fast become the trendiest spot in town with fine art galleries, great restau-

rants, unique shops, and antique stores. Central Station and the Arcade Restaurant border the south end, and the Orpheum Theatre sits to the north. Let the trolley drop you off for a festive lunch or a sophisticated dinner before a night at the theater. It's also nice for late-night entertainment. You're also invited to pop into the Memphis Heritage office at 509 South Main for a Historical Walking Tour.

Finally, the last Friday of every month features a free Trolley Night. Hop the trolley for an evening of music and fun while visiting all the galleries that stay open late.

delicious lunches and dinners (though the sophisticated menu, both in food and price, is not designed with youngsters in mind).

Victorian Village offers three homes that are open to the public: The modest Magevney House, which was built in 1836 and is the oldest middle-class structure in town. It was the home of one of the city's first school teachers. A wealthier world is represented at the Woodruff-Fontaine House, 680 Adams, which features a large collection of Victorian furnishings and 19th-century textiles. The Mallory-Neely House, 652 Adams, is a beautiful, Italian-style villa filled with original family furniture. (See separate listings for more details and the hours of operation for each home.) All three houses offer a fascinating glimpse into Memphis' past, with the requisite ghost stories to enhance the experience.

Viking Culinary Arts Center
119 South Main Street
578-5822, 877-3-VIKING
www.vikingrange.com
Open daily 10 a.m. – 6 p.m.

Viking is world-famous for its upscale kitchen appliances and utensils. This center features a world-class teaching kitchen, a theater demonstration kitchen, and a retail shop that offers professional-caliber cooking supplies as well as evening cooking classes. What's more, they offer cooking classes for kids throughout the year (length: 2 hours) as well as cooking camps during the summer (2-3 hours a day for 2 weeks). You can check the website for class schedules. Very cool.

W.C. Handy House Museum
352 Beale Street
527-3427
www.heritagetoursmemphis.com
Summer
Tuesday – Saturday:
10 a.m. – 5 p.m.

Winter
Tuesday – Saturday:
1 – 4 p.m.
Price: $2 for adults, $1 for youths
Tour length: 15-20 minutes

Recapture the atmosphere of early-20th-century Beale Street at the home of the "Father of the Blues." This modest, wood-frame house displays artifacts and memorabilia that depict the life of a musical innovator and legacy-maker. He introduced the world to the blues, and Beale Street is where it happened. His historic significance may be lost on small children, but they might indulge their parents' curiosity, since it's a relatively quick stop.

The innovative WONDERS series changed the way Memphians experience art, history, and culture. Its exhibitions attract hundreds of thousands of people because of their subject matter and their custom-built, architectural presentations. Past shows include "Titanic: The Exhibition," "Ramesses the Great," "Napoleon," and "Glory and Genius: Florence and the

WONDERS: THE ART OF THE MOTORCYCLE

WONDERS: Memphis International Cultural Series
The Pyramid Arena
1 Auction Avenue at Front Street
312-9161, 800-263-6744
www.wonders.org
April 22-October 30, 2005:
"The Art of the Motorcycle"
Open daily 9 a.m., entry every 15 minutes until 7 p.m.
Tour length: 1-2 hours
Price: $15 for adults, $7 for ages 5-12, free for 4 and under

Italian Renaissance."

The most current WONDERS exhibition revs up a unique display called "The Art of the Motorcycle." (It drew huge crowds when it premiered at New York's Guggenheim Museum.) It presents the history, evolution, and cultural impact of these motorized bikes from the earliest motorcycles (which preceded automobiles by 25 years) to the latest models. The exhibition focuses on aesthetics and design engineering, technological innovation, and the role of the motorcycle as a social and cultural icon symbolizing rebellion, freedom, danger, and more.

Woodruff-Fontaine House
680 Adams Avenue
526-1469
www.memphismuseums.org
Wednesday-Sunday:
noon – 4 p.m.
*Tours every half-hour
last tour at 3:30 p.m.
Closed Tuesdays
Price: $5 for adults, $4 for seniors, $3.50 for students
Tour length: 30 minutes

This fully restored, three-story French Victorian mansion was built in 1870. It is completely furnished with period furniture and accessories, and it includes a large collection of period clothing. Young girls may enjoy this more than young boys. However, the home's ghost stories seem to have universal appeal.

Kid-Friendly Restaurants
$ - $1 - $9
$$ - $10 - $19
$$$ - $20+

All of Memphis' downtown restaurants will gladly serve children (when accompanied by an adult). Most of the establishments on Beale Street, however, take on a decidedly more "bar-like" atmosphere after 9 p.m.

This is, of course, just a partial listing. I like many of the new ethnic restaurants that have opened in recent years, featuring the foods of India, Vietnam, Japan, and Russia. (Will is especially fond of Sawadii, a downtown Thai restaurant.) There are also a number of upscale restaurants that would offer not only delicious food but an opportunity for the kids to practice their dining Ps & Qs. Listed here, however, are more traditional eateries that will stir up the least resistance among picky eaters.

Arcade Restaurant - $
540 Beale Street
526-5757
Breakfast, lunch, & dinner. One of the city's oldest eateries and a favorite haunt of Elvis Presley. (You can sit in Elvis' favorite booth!) Big Southern breakfasts (served all day), plate lunches with Southern-style veggies. Super milkshakes. A personal favorite for breakfast with out-of-towners.

B.B. King's Blues Club - $$
143 Beale Street
524-5464
Lunch, dinner, bar, and live entertainment. Down-home Southern food and live entertainment seven nights a week. B.B. actually pops in to perform several times each year. With one of the best gift shops on Beale, this is the place for out-of-town guests. Best before 9 p.m.

B.B. KING'S BLUES CLUB

BLUES CITY CAFE

The Cupboard, Too - $
149 Madison Avenue
527-9111
Lunch & dinner. One of Memphis' most popular restaurants for home-cooked meals. Relaxed dining, with great rolls and desserts. A great way to make sure your kids get their vegetables (Southern-style).

Dan McGuinness Irish Pub - $-$$
150 Peabody Place
527-8500
Lunch & dinner (and bar). Authentic Irish pub. It was dismantled in Dublin and reassembled here. Good food, warm and cozy atmosphere. Live Celtic music on weekends.

Dyer's Burgers - $
205 Beale Street
527-DYER
Lunch & dinner (open late). Very casual. Retro '50s décor. And great *fried* burgers, cooked in grease first used in 1912. Milk shakes, coke floats.

> ### ∞ MEMPHIS TIDBIT
> Many Southerners refer to lunch as dinner. And dinner is called supper. For this guide, I call the noon-time meal "lunch" and the meal eaten after 5 p.m. as "dinner."

Blues City Café - $$
138 Beale Street
526-3637
Lunch & dinner, bar and live entertainment. Ribs, catfish, tamales, and gumbo. More adult-oriented after 9 p.m.

Café Fransisco - $
400 North Main Street
578-8002
Breakfast, lunch, & dinner. Located in the historic Pinch District, comfy & funky with DSL connections for the electronically inclined. Great coffees and smoothies, pastries and sandwiches. I like it for both breakfast and for lunch with friends (and children).

Cozy Corner - $
745 North Parkway
527-9158
10 a.m.- 7 p.m.
Tuesday -Saturday
I love this place, as do lots of the locals. Noted for its BBQ cornish hens, the BBQ ribs and pork sandwiches are also first-rate. Nothin' fancy but great food, served on paper plates with plastic cutlery. Finger-licking encouraged. It's also a smoke-free and alcohol-free environment. Owned by the Robinson family for more than 25 years. These are some of the nicest folks you'll ever meet, and the food is fantastic.

Front Street Deli - $
77 S. Front Street
522-8943
Breakfast & lunch. The best deli sandwiches in the world (my personal favorite: the hot-steamed ham and cheddar cheese). Grab'n'go or try your luck with the limited seating.

Gus's World Famous Hot & Spicy Chicken - $
310 South Front Street
527-4877
Lunch & dinner. As seen on the Food Network, this is a franchise location of the original Gus's (see Mason, Tennessee, in the regional

attractions section of this guide). The fried chicken here has a special flavor all its own, spicy, but not *too* spicy, and served with all the right trimmings.

Hard Rock Café - $-$$
315 Beale Street
523-0003
Lunch & dinner (bar & live entertainment). Classic American chow from burgers to brownies. Lots of musical memorabilia. Kids love these places worldwide.

Huey's Downtown - $
77 S. Second Street
527-2700
Lunch & dinner (bar & live entertainment). Any and all Memphians will tell you this is the best burger in town. The potato soup is pretty fabulous, too. Graffiti is encouraged, and most importantly, ask your server for some toothpicks for the "frill-pick shooting" into the ceilings. Voted "Most Kid-Friendly" in *Memphis* magazine's reader's poll.

Isaac Hayes Music Food Passion - $$
150 Peabody Place
529-9222
Lunch & dinner (bar & live entertainment). BBQ ribs, meatloaf, and soul-food specialties. Good food, stylish place. Kids will do fine for lunch, but I recommend older children for supper. And, yes, you might see Isaac himself. (For the younger members of your clan who may not remember the Oscar-winning *Shaft* connection, just tell 'em that Isaac Hayes and the voice of Chef from TV's *South Park* are one and the same. That ought to impress them.)

Jillian's - $-$$
150 Peabody Place
543-8800
Lunch & dinner (and bar). On the main floor is the video café and "power bar" with a lot to choose from on the menu. The adjacent

Nine Ball Lounge offers billiards and there's an Atlas Dance Club, too. Downstairs you'll find the Hi Life Bowling Lanes. My son loves this. It's very cool. On the second floor, you'll find more "snack dining" in the Amazing Game Room: With 150 games, your kids will go wild. Best for lunch or early dinner. It gets a bit wild and loud as the evening wears on.

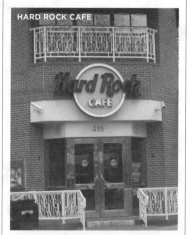

also a sure kid-pleaser. Shrimp, lobster, crawfish and crab, plus chicken, steak, and pasta, with children's portions available. Indoor playground and arcade area. Indoor and outdoor seating overlooking the Mississippi River.

Little Tea Shop - $
69 Monroe Avenue
525-0742
Lunch only. Practically an institution, this is a longtime, solid favorite with the locals. Delicious vegetables and daily specials plus soups, salads, and sandwiches. Also offers Middle Eastern cuisine. Simple, family-friendly, and for basketball fans, there's a bonus: lots of photos and autographs of high-profile hoopsters.

Maggie Moo's Ice Cream & Treatery - $
150 Peabody Place
205-1011
Breakfast, lunch, & dinner. More

THE LITTLE TEA SHOP

Joe's Crab Shack/ Eat at Joe's - $$
263 Wagner Place
526-1966
Lunch & dinner (bar & live entertainment). Yes, it's a chain, but it's

than 40 flavors of homemade, premium ice cream churned daily. Cakes, shakes, malts, floats, sundaes, real fruit smoothies plus Maggie Moo's celebrated Memphis Grits. Great burgers, too!

NEELY'S BARBECUE

CHARLIE VERGOS' RENDEZVOUS

Neely's Barbecue - $-$$
670 Jefferson Avenue
521-9798
Lunch & dinner. One of the city's most popular BBQ restaurants (and you know it's good if it's a favorite of the natives). Try their low-fat turkey BBQ. They even offer BBQ spaghetti! Friendly service, too.
* *The Neely family also owns a BBQ restaurant at 2265 S. Third (known as Interstate Bar-B-Q), plus two other locations farther east.*

Pat O'Brien's - $$
310 Beale Street
529-0900
Lunch & dinner. The only Pat O'Brien's outside of New Orleans. Children welcome for lunch and dinner, though it takes on a more adult "flavor" after 9 p.m. Same food and famous beverages as the original. Live entertainment.

Peanut Shoppe - $
24 Main Street
525-1115
All snacks, all day. Roasted peanuts, snow cones, and candy, right on the trolley route.

Rendezvous (Charlie Vergos' Rendezvous) - $$
52 South Second Street
(down an alley across from the Peabody Hotel)
523-2746
Dinner. Memphis' most famous BBQ restaurant. Very casual, overflowing with memorabilia, and famous for its dry ribs. Kids and grownups love this place. Be sure to ask for a sausage-and-cheese plate.

Spaghetti Warehouse - $-$$
40 Huling Avenue
521-0907
Lunch & dinner (and bar). Tucked (actually hidden) just west of Front Street, kids love this place not only because it offers all the usual favorites (spaghetti, chicken fingers, burgers, etc.), but because many of the seating areas are inside old train cars. Yes, actual train cars. The whole place is casual, full of memorabilia, and fun.

Kid-Friendly Hotels

Of course, there are lots of perfectly nice hotels, but when I'm traveling with our kids, a pool is a must, preferably heated or indoor for year-round convenience. I've also learned to appreciate the privacy and space offered by a suites hotel. So here are a few recommendations based on these personal biases, with a warning: Downtown hotels are a bit pricey compared to those in other areas.

$	-	$40-$59
$$	-	$60-$89
$$$	-	$90-$189
$$$$	-	$190+

Comfort Inn - $$
100 North Front Street
526-0583, 800-228-5150
www.comfortinn.com/hotel/tn235
This hotel does not have a heated or indoor pool, but in the hot summer months, it's cool to swim in the rooftop pool overlooking the Mississippi River. Fitness center, restaurant. Just a few blocks from Beale Street and AutoZone Park.

Hampton Inn & Suites – Peabody Place - $$$
175 Peabody Place
260-4000, 800-HAMPTON
www.hampton-inn.com
Indoor heated pool, fitness center, and complimentary continental breakfast. Borders Beale Street and Peabody Place. Close to AutoZone Park.

Holiday Inn Select
Downtown - $$$
160 Union Avenue
525-5491, 888-300-5491
www.hisdowntownmemphis.com
Outdoor heated pool, fitness center, restaurant, and room service. Union Café and Sekisui Sushi Bar. Two blocks from Beale Street, one block from AutoZone Park.

The Madison Hotel - $$$$
79 Madison Avenue
333-1200, 866-44-MEMPHIS
www.madisonhotelmemphis.com
Indoor heated pool, fitness center, fine restaurant and room service, sophisticated bar. Upscale, luxury accommodations with convenient location. Hotel's restaurant, Grill 83, and bar are popular with the after-work crowd. Best suited for older teens and young adults.

Memphis Marriott
Downtown - $$$
250 North Main Street
527-7300, 888-557-8740
www.marriott.com/memdt
Indoor heated pool, fitness center, restaurant, room service, and bar. Large, convention hotel located at trolley station (short trolley ride to all Downtown attractions).

The Peabody Hotel - $$$$
149 Union Avenue
529-4000, 800-PEABODY
www.peabodymemphis.com
Indoor heated pool, fitness center, restaurants, room service, famous lobby bar — and the Peabody Ducks. Includes the upscale restaurant, Capriccio, and the very, very upscale restaurant, Chez Philippe.

The Radisson Downtown - $$$
185 Union Avenue
528-1800, 800-333-3333
www.radisson.com
Outdoor, *unheated* pool and jacuzzi, fitness center, restaurant and room service, bar. Directly across the street from AutoZone Park and just two blocks from Beale Street.

Sleep Inn at Court Square - $$
40 North Front Street
522-9700, 800-4CHOICE
www.sleepinn.com
No pool, but there is a fitness center. Complimentary continental breakfast. Overlooks quaint Court Square at trolley stop. Easy walk to Beale Street and AutoZone Park.

Spring Hill Suites
Court Square - $$$
21 North Main Street
522-2100, 888-287-9400
www.springhillsuites.com
Outdoor heated pool and fitness center, complimentary continental breakfast. Next to the Sleep Inn, overlooking historic Court Square near the trolley stop. Short walk to many downtown attractions.

Talbot Heirs - $$$
99 South Second Street
527-9772, 800-955-3956
www.talbothouse.com
Very handsome, comfortable, and "happenin'." Some rooms have their own fitness equipment. Complimentary breakfast in suite. Best for teens and young adults. Though designed more for business travelers, the owners are sympathetic to children as they have three of their own. No restaurant, but they will stock the fully equipped kitchen if you send them a list.

THE PEABODY HOTEL

CHAPTER 3

Midtown

Where it all comes together

THE MEMPHIS ZOO

I LOVE MIDTOWN Memphis. I grew up here. It is a microcosm of the whole city, a wonderful blend of "Old Memphis" (meaning social prominence), the fringe, and the funky, students and academics. There are Arts-and-Crafts bungalows that serve as starter homes for young families. There are stately mansions on boulevards lined with massive, century-old trees. And there are some areas that have seen better days. This place was diverse long before it was politically correct.

For longtime Memphians (those whose families have been around for several generations),

Midtown is defined as "within the Parkways." This means that it is the area east of downtown but west of East Parkway. It is south of North Parkway and north of South Parkway. Are you still with me? But the city limits have expanded dramatically in the past 50 years, and for the purposes of this book, we'll stay within North Parkway and South Parkway, but we'll go farther east to Highland Avenue.

Midtown is a mixed bag that includes several major colleges and universities. It is primarily residential, but includes a lot of commercial areas as well. There are neighborhood eateries, grand

churches, popular museums, and great antique shops. Perhaps most notably, you'll find beautiful Overton Park in Midtown, which is home to the Memphis Zoo, Memphis Brooks Museum of Art, Memphis College of Art, a golf course, hiking trails, and picnic areas. Overton Park was featured prominently in Peter Taylor's story "The Old Forest." Midtown is or once was home to another couple of writers of note: Shelby Foote and Tennessee Williams, who wrote his first play here.

A popular bumper sticker declares "Midtown is Memphis," and I tend to agree.

Sites & Attractions

Art Museum of the University of Memphis
3750 Norriswood (on campus)
678-2224, 800-669-2678
www.amum.org
Monday – Saturday: 9 a.m. – 5 p.m.
Closed university holidays and
while changing exhibitions
Price: Free
Tour length: 45 minutes

This is a relatively small but well-organized museum with a number of interesting items that are worth seeing. There are permanent displays of Egyptian antiquities and West African artifacts along with changing exhibitions of contemporary art.

If you have a child who is interested in art or Egyptian or African culture, you might want to include this in your itinerary.

Children's Museum of Memphis
2525 Central Avenue
458-4033
www.cmom.com
Tuesday–Saturday: 9 a.m.–5 p.m.
Sunday: noon - 5 p.m.
Closed Mondays and
some holidays
Price: $7 for adults, $6 for ages 1-12 and 62+, free for 1 year and under
Tour length: 2 hours

This discovery museum, always popular with the younger set, recently completed a multi-million-dollar expansion to add exhibits that appeal to older children, too. The museum is filled with hands-on, interactive displays, including a child-sized city, WaterWorks!, Art Smart, and the cockpit of a real airplane.

Will, now in his teens, and his friends loved this place as tots but seemed to outgrow it as they got older. I was eager to see Will's reaction to the expansion when we went back for a recent visit. While he said he still thought it was best for "littler kids," I noticed he had a great time, and the new exhibits managed to keep him occupied for a good hour. Additionally, he still wanted to revisit some of his favorite exhibits "from his youth."

Cooper-Young Entertainment District
South Cooper at Young Avenue
276-7222
www.cooperyoung.com

This retail district offers a pleasant diversion for a meal and a little shopping. There are several restaurants and coffeehouses, plus a few galleries and gift shops for those with artsy taste and interests. It has a kind of bohemian feel to it, nestled within an old, modest neighborhood. It's frequented by artists, students, college professors, and "old Memphis" types, too. Some of the eateries are casual and inexpensive, but finer dining is also available here.

Laser Quest
3417 Plaza Drive
(Poplar Plaza Shopping Center)
324-4800
www.laserquest.com
Tuesday – Thursday: 6 p.m. – 10 p.m.
Friday: 4 p.m. – midnight
Saturday: noon – midnight
Sunday: 1 p.m. – 8 p.m.
Price: $7 per game, $6 with a group of 10 or more

Yes, this is like many "entertainment chains" around the country, but most kids love it (though I think it's too intense for kids under 5). Laser Quest combines tag and hide 'n' seek with, what else, laser guns. It's great for rainy days or for kids who like live action experiences.

P.S. Don't wear white; it glows in the dark, making you an easy target for the opposing team.

Libertyland Amusement Park
940 Early Maxwell Boulevard
(Fairgrounds)
274-1776, 800-552-PARK
www.libertyland.com
Late April – early June and mid-August – Labor Day weekend:
Saturday: 10 a.m. – 8 p.m.
Sunday: Noon – 8 p.m.
Early June – mid-August:
Wednesday – Friday: Noon – 8 p.m.
Saturday: 10 a.m. – 8 p.m.
Sunday: Noon – 8 p.m.
General admission: $8
Thrill Ride wristband:
$10, free under
age 3 and over age 55
Length of stay: 3-4 hours
Food on-site.
NOTE: Seasonal hours, not open during winter months

CHILDREN'S MUSEUM OF MEMPHIS

An amusement park in the heart of town. Libertyland offers 24 rides (including *two* roller coasters) for small children as well as big kids, plus live entertainment, carnival games (for which you'll need extra cash), and the requisite funnel cakes, pronto pups (which were invented in Memphis), and smoothies.

Libertyland is big enough to offer lots of serious fun for all ages, but it's not so large that it's overwhelming or takes all day to enjoy. It's a perfect size, and the crowds are not bad, except during the annual Mid-South Fair in September, when it's *very* crowded.

Memphis Brooks Museum of Art
1934 Poplar Avenue
(in Overton Park)
544-6200
www.brooksmuseum.org
Tuesday – Friday: 10 a.m. – 4 p.m.
Saturday: 10 a.m. – 5 p.m.
Sunday: 11:30 a.m. – 5 p.m.
Closed Monday
Price: $6 for adults, $5 for seniors, $2 for students, under 6 free
Tour length: 1 hour
Restaurant on-site

One of the South's finest museums with one of the region's largest collections, Brooks exhibits fine art from antiquities to contemporary works. Its permanent collection includes Renaissance and Baroque paintings and sculpture, European and American paintings, African art, and more. Brooks also hosts international traveling exhibitions, many of which are particularly kid-friendly and fun.

After an hour or so of meandering through the various galleries, I like to have lunch at the museum's Brushmark restaurant. It's especially nice to sit outdoors overlooking the park, weather permitting. The kids might find the inside restaurant a bit stuffy but should enjoy sitting outside.

One last thing: great shopping. I get lots of family gifts in the gift shop and bookstore. There are some fun things for children to purchase too.

∽ MEMPHIS TIDBIT
In addition to having one of the country's finest, hand-crafted carrousels, Libertyland also boasts one of the country's oldest remaining wooden roller-coasters, the famous Zippin Pippin — Elvis' favorite ride.

MEMPHIS BROOKS MUSEUM OF ART

MEMPHIS PINK PALACE MUSEUM

Memphis Pink Palace Museum
3050 Central Avenue
320-6320
www.memphismuseums.org
Tuesday – Saturday: 9 a.m. – 5 p.m.
Sunday: noon – 5 p.m.
closed Monday
Price: $8 for adults, $7.50 for seniors, $5.50 for ages 3-12
Tour length: 2 hours
Restaurant on-site

Tennessee's most visited museum, the Pink Palace includes a regional history museum, IMAX theater, and the Sharpe Planetarium* — all under one roof. When I was a child, the museum was located inside the Pink Palace mansion, which was built by Clarence Saunders (the man who first developed the self-service grocery store, Piggly Wiggly). The 1920s mansion is still open to the public, but the primary exhibit areas are now found in the more recent additions. Favorite exhibits include the shrunken head, the mind-boggling miniature circus, life-sized history dioramas, dinosaur displays, and a replica of the first Piggly Wiggly.

The Sharpe Planetarium (separate admission charges: $4.25 for adults, $3.75 for seniors and children 3-12) offers a variety of multi-media astronomy programs and laser shows.

The Pink Palace also hosts holiday-themed events, including the annual Enchanted Forest and Festival of Trees.

Will and his friends never tire of this place. It appeals to all ages, with the rotating exhibits and IMAX movies ensuring that each visit feels new and different. Their gift shop is first-rate too.
* *Call before going. City budget cuts may dictate hours of operation.*

Memphis Zoo
2200 Prentiss Place
(in Overton Park)
276-WILD
www.memphiszoo.org
March-October: 9 a.m. – 6 p.m.
November – February: 9 a.m. – 5 p.m.
Last admission: One hour before closing
Closed some holidays
Price: $10 for adults, $9 for seniors, $6 for ages 2-11
Children under 2 are free
Tour length: 2-3 hours
Restaurant on-site

Truly one of the finest zoos in the country, its grand Egyptian-themed entry gives you a hint of the surprises within. More than 3,000 animals reside here, many of them in unique, natural, free-roaming environments. Over $30 million has been spent in recent years creating such areas as Cat

Country, Primate Canyon, Animals of the Night (a particular favorite), Once Upon a Farm, the Tropical Bird House, and the China exhibit, which now houses a rare pair of pandas: Ya Ya and Le Le. (Ya Ya and Le Le have taken the region by storm — and they really are charming. Kids of all ages love them.) The zoo also offers year-round special programs and animal shows.

Overton Square Entertainment District
Madison Avenue at Cooper
273-0014
www.overtonsquare.com

This multi-block entertainment district features a variety of restaurants, an assortment of retail shops, the live theater of Playhouse on the Square, live entertainment venues, and one of the region's hippest movie theaters. It's a convenient, one-stop spot that can occupy several hours.

Union Planters IMAX Theatre
Located at the Pink Palace Museum
3050 Central Avenue
320-6320
www.memphismuseums.org
Open seven days a week, seasonal hours
Price: $7.25 for adults, $6.75 for seniors, $5.75 for ages 3-12
Movie lengths: 1 hour
Restaurant on-site

Have you met a kid who *didn't* like an IMAX movie? A giant, four-story screen offers crystal-clear images and sharp, digital surround sound. You do more than see the movies; you *feel* them.
NOTE: Call in advance for show times and reservations.

Kid-Friendly Restaurants
$ - $1 - $9
$$ - $10 - $19
$$$ - $20+

Anderton's - $$
1901 Madison Avenue
726-4010
Lunch (except on Saturday) & dinner, bar. Closed on Sunday. Casual. Seafood and steaks (great rolls). 1960s underwater décor, including vintage diving suit.

The Bar-B-Q Shop - $-$$
1782 Madison Avenue
272-1277
Lunch & dinner. Real pit BBQ with BBQ sandwiches on Texas toast, dry ribs, spaghetti. Bar. Live entertainment.

Barksdale Restaurant - $
237 South Cooper
722-2193
Breakfast & lunch. Neighborhood staple, especially for big, hot breakfasts (eggs, pancakes, you name it) and Southern-style lunches with lots of veggies, rolls, fried chicken, and desserts (like a really terrific banana pudding).

Boscos Squared - $$
2120 Madison Avenue
432-2222
Lunch & dinner. Home of famous Flaming Stone Beer. Brewery tours available. European wood-fired oven pizza, grilled meat and seafood, sandwiches, vegetarian dishes. Sunday jazz brunch.

Brother Juniper's College Inn - $
3519 Walker Avenue
324-0144
Tuesday – Friday: 6:30 a.m.–1 p.m.
Saturday: 7 a.m. – 12:30 p.m.
Breakfast & lunch. A great way to start the day with super breakfasts and terrific pastries. Near the University of Memphis, this is a local favorite because of its good food and casual atmosphere. Very family-friendly.

YA YA AT THE MEMPHIS ZOO

CAFÉ OLÉ

something with a French country flair. Delicious crepes, popovers, and divine desserts. Upscale but kid-friendly.

Sekisui - $-$$
25 South Belvedere Boulevard
725-0005
Lunch & dinner. The atmosphere is casual and relaxed. My youngest loves the chicken teriyaki and is quite proud of his mastery of chopsticks. All ages enjoy watching the little sushi boats that glide on the "river" that circles around the center of the restaurant.

Young Avenue Deli - $
2119 Young Avenue
278-0034
Lunch & dinner. *USA Today* ranked its French fries as the third best in the U.S.A. Readers of *The Memphis Flyer* voted the Young Avenue Deli as Memphis' "Best Place to See Live Music."

Zinnie's East – $-$$
1718 Madison Avenue
274-7101
Lunch & dinner. Casual. Chicken, burgers, salads, pastas, veggie plates. When the weather's good, you can sit on the small front deck.

Kid-Friendly Hotels

Midtown doesn't have as many full-service hotels to choose from as Downtown, and they cater more to business travelers. I am recommending one, however, because it is conveniently located and has many of the amenities that keep kids happy.

$	-	$40-$59
$$	-	$60-$89
$$$	-	$90-$189
$$$$	-	$190+

French Quarter Suites Hotel - $$
2144 Madison Avenue
728-4000, 800-843-0353
www.memphisfrenchquarter.com
All suites. Full-service restaurant and room service. Outdoor, *unheated* pool and fitness center.

Brother Juniper's at the Palace Restaurant - $
3050 Central Avenue
(inside Pink Palace Museum)
320-6407
Breakfast & lunch. Same delicious oven-baked pastries, breads and granolas, salads, sandwiches, soups, and desserts as the Walker Avenue location, but a more limited menu.

Café Olé - $
959 South Cooper
274-1504
Lunch & dinner. Homemade recipes of Southwestern beef, chicken, shrimp, and vegetarian meals. Sandwiches and salads. Casual atmosphere.

The Cupboard - $
1400 Union Avenue
276-8015
Lunch & dinner. Home-cooked meals with lots of Southern veggies and meats, and killer desserts.

Huey's – Midtown (The original) - $
1927 Madison Avenue
726-4372
Lunch & dinner. Home of the famous "Huey Burger," Memphis' best. Chicken fingers, steak kabobs, salads, and soups. The kids will want to test their skills at frill-pick shooting and sanctioned graffiti scrawling. Live music on Sundays.

Java Cabana - $
2170 Young Avenue
272-7210
Lunch & dinner. Coffeehouse featuring Seattle's Best coffee, 1950s décor, special events, and live music.

Otherlands Café - $
641 South Cooper
278-4994
Breakfast & lunch. Non-smoking café and exotic gift shop. Coffee, espresso drinks, fresh-squeezed juices, breads and pastries, homemade pies, and vegan goodies. Lots of artsy types and occasional live entertainment.

Paulette's - $$$
2110 Madison Avenue
726-5128
Lunch & dinner. For something a little different than blue jeans and burgers, dress up the offspring for

CHAPTER 4

East Memphis

Not quite the 'burbs, but close

GREAT OUTDOORS FESTIVAL

EAST MEMPHIS is best known for its handsome, mostly upscale residential areas and for its abundance of shopping options. Years ago, Memphis' eastern limit was determined by I-240, but now it extends several more miles, sharing boundaries with the cities of Germantown and Cordova.

Three main arteries cut through East Memphis, heading west to east: Walnut Grove Road, Poplar Avenue, and Park Avenue. Poplar Avenue actually begins at the Mississippi River, runs all the way through town, and continues through the next several towns (past Germantown, Collierville, and as far as La Grange, Tennessee). Poplar is probably the most heavily traveled street in Memphis, but it's an effective reference point. You can find just about any place in town from it, but be prepared for delays, and allow yourself extra time for travel.

That said, there are several attractions, shops, and eateries on or near Poplar Avenue, especially "out East" (as the natives refer to it). Audubon Park (on Goodlett between Park and Southern) offers golf, hiking, and picnicking amenities, and it's adjacent to the Memphis Botanic Garden. Just across the street is the Dixon Gallery and Gardens, and you're just minutes from the Oak Court Shopping Mall, Eastgate and Laurelwood Shopping Centers, a top-of-the-line movie complex called Paradiso, and many popular restaurants. An extra amenity: lots of convenient parking.

Sites & Attractions

Agricenter International

7777 Walnut Grove Road
757-7777
www.agricenter.org
Tour length: Depends on event
Price: Many events are free; other costs vary

Established as an agricultural research, development, and resource center, the "Ag Center" has become the site of many special events throughout the year that are enjoyed by the entire community. In the spring, families are invited to pick their own strawberries from the 13-acre field off Walnut Grove Road. Throughout the warm months, Mid-Southerners visit the Farmer's Market, located inside the Center's Red Barn, for a vast selection of fresh-from-the-fields fruits and vegetables. (I always leave with more than I need because it all looks so enticing.) Each fall, thousands of people challenge themselves by trying to find their way out of the huge corn maze (a sure bet for a great family outing, especially as Halloween approaches and the maze becomes haunted). The Shelby Showcase Arena, site of year-round events (especially for equestrians) is adjacent to the Center. Call or check online to see what's up; there's almost always something.

LICHTERMAN NATURE CENTER

Cordova Cellars
(Cordova area/extreme
East Memphis)
9050 Macon Road
754-3442
Tuesday – Saturday: 10 a.m. – 5 p.m.
Sunday: 1 p.m. – 5 p.m.
Price: Free
Tour length: 45 minutes

No, Napa Valley and Upstate New York can't claim all the wine for themselves. Cordova Cellars is a full-production winery in a beautiful, rural setting. Open for tours, tastings, and sales, you're invited to visit the cellar to learn how wine is made, then sample for yourself. There are also picnic areas, and frequently guests are treated to live entertainment.

Crystal Shrine Grotto
at Memorial Park Cemetery
5668 Poplar Avenue
767-8930
Open 7 days a week: 8 a.m. – 4 p.m.
Price: Free
Tour length: 30 minutes

The Memorial Park Cemetery is indeed more like a park, and with-

DIXON GALLERY AND GARDENS

in this shady expanse, you can follow the signs that lead to the Crystal Shrine Grotto — a hidden treasure that even many Memphians don't know exists. In the late 1930s, a cave was constructed by the cemetery founder, Clovis Hinds, and the Mexican artist, Dionicio Rodriquez. While the outside of the cavern is made of concrete that looks like rocks, the inside contains the real thing: natural rock and quartz crystal, brought in from the Ozark Mountains, which serve as backdrops for sculptures depicting nine scenes of the life of Jesus. It really does feel magical.

Dixon Gallery and Gardens
4339 Park Avenue
761-5250
www.dixon.org
Tuesday – Saturday: 10 a.m. – 5 p.m.
Sunday: 1 p.m. – 5 p.m.
Closed Monday
Price: $5
Tour length: 1-2 hours

Once a private estate belonging to the Dixon family, this museum is dedicated primarily to Impressionist and post–Impressionist paintings. It also contains a beautiful collection of 18th-century porcelain and features changing exhibitions as well. The original home is surrounded by 17 acres of formal and informal gardens that are colorful year-round. Special events are held on the grounds during the warm months, including picnics and concerts, most notably with the Memphis Symphony Orchestra. In the fall, Dixon hosts Shakespeare in the Gardens, a performance by the Shenandoah Shakespeare Express. Dixon also has a fine gift shop which features beautiful jewelry among its wares.

Lichterman Nature Center

5992 Quince Road
767-7322
www.memphismuseums.org
Monday – Thursday: 9 a.m. – 4 p.m.
Friday – Saturday: 9 a.m. – 5 p.m.
Price: $6 for adults
$4.50 for ages 3-12
Tour length: 2 hours

It always amazes me to find such an abundance of woods and wildlife in the middle of a large city, but that's exactly what Lichterman has to offer.

Lichterman was the first accredited nature center in the U.S. Its latest renovation added a Backyard Wildlife Center, which features an environmental lab that changes with the seasons and offers hands-on exploration of wildlife. It also includes a 240-foot-long Forest Boardwalk that leads to a teaching platform in a tree canopy. In addition, you'll find a Visitor's Center,

PUTT-PUTT FAMILY PARK

nature store, special events pavilion, greenhouse, boardwalks, and trails that wind past a forest, lake, and meadow. Tuesdays from 1 to 4 p.m., admission is free. The last tickets are sold one hour prior to closing.

Malco Summer Quartet Drive-In Theater

5310 Summer Avenue
767-4320
Open 7 days a week during summer
Box office opens at 7:45 p.m.
Shows begin at 8:45 p.m.
Open weekends during spring & fall
Price: $6 for adults, kids 11 and under free
Concessions on-site

A rare bit of Americana — a real drive-in movie! If your kids have never been to one, then you need to get moving. Very few of these places are left in the country, so this is a rare treat. The Summer Quartet Drive-In is Tennessee's largest, offering double features on each of its four screens. For those of you who have not been to a drive-in since the '60s or '70s, there are a few modern updates (you don't put those clunky talk boxes on your window anymore, you tune in on your radio instead), but it still captures all the same fun. **NOTE:** Take plenty of mosquito repellent!

Memphis Botanic Garden

750 Cherry Road
685-1566
www.memphisbotanicgarden.com
March – October:
Monday – Saturday: 9 a.m. – 6 p.m.
Sunday: 11 a.m. – 6 p.m.
November – February:
Monday – Saturday:
9 a.m. – 4:30 p.m.
Sunday: 11 a.m. – 4:30 p.m.
Price: $5 for adults, $4 for seniors, $3 for children 3-12
Tour length: 1-2 hours

The Memphis Botanic Garden features 22 gardens covering 96 acres, including a sensory garden for the blind and a Japanese garden. There are also gardens for wildflowers, sculpture, organic, perennials, and cactus, plus dogwood and azalea trails. In addition to walking tours, motorized trams are available.

The Goldsmith Civic Garden Center features a porcelain collec-

tion, tropical conservatory, horticulture shows, and special events.

Putt-Putt Family Park

5484 Summer Avenue
386-2992
www.puttputtmemphis.com
Sunday – Thursday:
8 a.m. - midnight
Friday – Saturday: 8 a.m. – 1 a.m.
Closes one hour earlier during the school year
Price: Each attraction is ticketed separately, wristbands available
Snack bar on-site

If your child can't have fun here, it's time to go back home. Putt-Putt is a 40-acre park with kiddie rides, a golf driving range, batting cages, miniature golf, go-karts, laser tag, bumper boats, a virtual roller-coaster, and a game room/arcade. Players win tickets that are redeemable for souvenirs. Need I say more?

Shelby Farms

7171 Mullins Station Road
382-2249
www.shelbycountytn.gov
Open year-round, sunrise to sunset

The largest urban park in the U.S., Shelby Farms spans 4,500 acres. If your offspring need to run off some energy, this is the place. It's pretty unusual to see bison grazing anywhere, especially within a city's limits, but you'll find a herd of bison here, and there's a Longhorn range, too. Patriot Lake and Chickasaw Lake both offer hiking trails (8 miles of paved trails) plus canoeing and sailing. Naturally, there are picnic areas, as well as roller-blading trails, a BMX track, a Tour de Wolf bike trail, a shooting range, and an archery range. Shelby Farms hosts a popular summer concert series, too, which attracts big-name performers. Special mounted rangers provide friendly information as well as security. You can be entertained here for days. Shooting and archery ranges: 377-4635

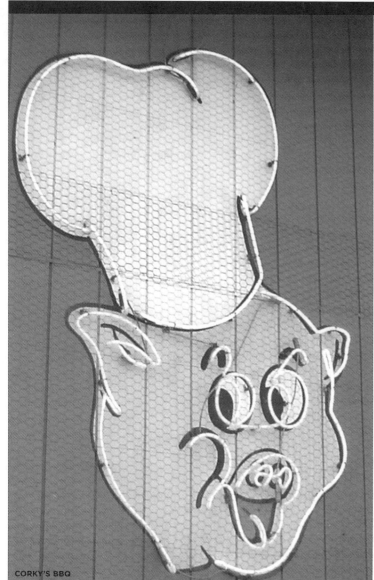

CORKY'S BBQ

The Half Shell - $-$$
688 S. Mendenhall
682-3966
Lunch & dinner. Casual atmosphere. Crab, oysters, steaks, chicken, and sandwiches.

Houston's - $$
5000 Poplar Avenue
683-0915
Go early or at off-hours to avoid a long wait. (Sundays from 1 to 3 p.m., it's packed.) Lunch & dinner. A big menu with lots to choose from and large portions. Super selection of desserts. Kids love it as much as the grownups.

Huey's - $
Two Locations:
4872 Poplar Avenue
682-7729
1771 Germantown Parkway
754-3885
Lunch & dinner. Same terrific Huey's as described in virtually every chapter of this book.

Memphis Pizza Café - $
Three of four Locations:
5061 Park Avenue
684-1306
7004 W. Farmington Boulevard
753-8218
8385 Highway 64
380-3888
Lunch & dinner. One of four locations offering homemade pizzas baked on brick slates, salads, and sandwiches in a casual, family-style setting.

Kid-Friendly Restaurants
$ - $1 - $9
$$ - $10 - $19
$$$ - $20+

Benihana - $$
912 Ridge Lake Boulevard
683-7390
Lunch & dinner. Every city has one, and kids love it. Good food, entertaining chefs.

Corky's BBQ - $-$$
5255 Poplar Avenue
685-9744
Lunch & dinner. One of Memphis' best BBQ shops, featuring wet and dry ribs, with pork BBQ sandwiches, and BBQ chicken. Beware: big crowds; go early or be prepared to wait. (There is another Corky's in the Cordova area/extreme East Memphis: 1740 Germantown Parkway, 737-1911.)

Dixie Café - $-$$
4699 Poplar Avenue
683-7555
Lunch & dinner. Southern downhome cooking. Yummy rolls and desserts (especially the banana pudding). One of three locations.

HUEY'S

Lunch & dinner — except no lunch on Saturday. Like Shoguns everywhere: good food, entertaining service, kids' portions, and kid-pleasing.

Wild Oats - $
5022 Poplar Avenue
685-2293
Lunch & dinner. Deli-style "whole foods" and vegetarian dishes. Pizza, hot-food bar, salad bar, deli, juice and coffee bar.

Kid-Friendly Hotels
$	-	$40-$59
$$	-	$60-$89
$$$	-	$90-$189
$$$$	-	$190+

There are more than 75 hotels in East Memphis and neighboring communities, and children are welcome at all of them.

Neely's Bar-B-Que Restaurant - $- $$
5700 Mt. Moriah
795-4177
Lunch & dinner. Same great BBQ, different location.
FUN FACT: Al Roker of the *Today* show loves Neely's BBQ

Owen Brennan's - $$
6150 Poplar Avenue
761-0990
Lunch & dinner. Cajun, Creole, and seafood in upscale New Orleans style. Maybe not a kid's first choice, but the food is good, and it's the only Brennan's outside of New Orleans. Live jazz on weekends.

Pancho's - $
2841 South Perkins Road
363-8118
Lunch & dinner. This is just one of several locations. Casual, kid-friendly Mexican fare. More trivia: This chain began in West Memphis, Arkansas, where the original restaurant is still in operation.

Shogun Japanese Restaurant - $$
(*Cordova area, extreme East Memphis*)
2314 Germantown Parkway
384-4122

THE DIXIE CAFÉ

However, many of these properties cater more to the business traveler. I have selected several to recommend with which I am personally familiar. I also included a few limited-service properties for a choice of budget options.

Doubletree – $$$
(formerly the Hilton East Memphis)
5069 Sanderlin Avenue
767-6666
www.doubletree.com
Upscale hotel with full-service restaurant, outdoor pool, heated indoor pool, and a fitness center.

Embassy Suites Memphis - $$$
1022 S. Shady Grove Road
684-1777, 800-EMBASSY
www.hilton.com
Heated indoor pool, fitness center, game room, and free cooked-to-order breakfast. Always a winner when traveling with children.

Hampton Inn and Suites - $$
962 S. Shady Grove Road
762-0056, 800-HAMPTON
www.hamptoninn.com
One of 10 Hampton Inn properties, one of three hotels with suites. Room service, heated outdoor pool, fitness center.

Hilton Hotel - $$$
(formerly the Park Vista and Adam's Mark)
939 Ridge Lake Boulevard
684-6664
www.hilton.com
Large, high-rise hotel with heated outdoor pool, fitness center, restaurant, and room service.

Holiday Inn Express Hotel & Suites - $$
4225 American Way
369-8005
www.Holiday-Inn.com
Heated indoor pool, gym, and complimentary continental breakfast. Birthday parties welcome (pizza deliveries also welcome).

Holiday Inn Select – East - $$$
5795 Poplar Avenue
682-7881, 800-HOLIDAY
www.holiday-inn.com/
mem-mtmoriah
Heated indoor pool and fitness center. Hotel features restaurant with room service.

Memphis Marriott East - $$
2625 Thousand Oaks Boulevard
362-6200, 800-627-3587
www.marriotthotels.com/memtn
Outdoor pool and heated indoor pool, plus fitness center, restaurant, and room service; 20 minutes from most major attractions.

HILTON HOTEL

CHAPTER 5

South Memphis and Airport Area

From Native American to native son

ELVIS' GRAVESITE AND MEDITATION GARDEN

WHILE MOST OF MEMPHIS' most famous attractions are concentrated downtown or in the heart of the city, South Memphis and the airport areas each have their own draws. In fact, the largest draw of all — Graceland — is a mere 10-minute drive from the airport, making it all the more convenient for the thousands of tourists from all parts of the globe who make the pilgrimage to the King's former castle.

South Memphis

Chucalissa Archaeological Museum
1987 Indian Village Drive
785-3160
www.chucalissa.org
Tuesday – Saturday: 9 a.m. – 5 p.m.
Sunday: 1 – 5 p.m.
Closed Monday
Price: $5 for adults, $3 for seniors and children under 11
Tour length: 45 minutes, last admission time is 4:30 p.m.

A visit to this historical attraction is one of Memphis' most authentic experiences. Built on a Native-American temple mound complex, Chucalissa features Native-American artifacts centered around a reconstructed, pre-Columbian village dating back to 1000 A.D.

I can remember visiting Chucalissa as a child with a sense of awe and mystery. Over the years, the museum expanded and became more sophisticated and informa-

tive. However, I was a bit disappointed when I took my son Will in 2004. I'd heard that the museum, which is supported by the University of Memphis, was at the mercy of some major funding cuts and, regrettably, it was evident. The good news is that it has a new executive director, and some new fund-raising initiatives are underway. (I so hope that this treasure endures; I mailed in a donation just a few days after my visit.) In the meantime, it is still a worthwhile experience and an excellent learning opportunity.

Airport Area

Graceland
3734 Elvis Presley Boulevard
332-3322, 800-238-2000
www.elvis.com
March – October:
Monday – Saturday: 9 a.m. – 5 p.m.
Sunday: 10 a.m. – 4 p.m.
November – February:
Open daily: 10 a.m. – 4 p.m.
Closed Tuesdays
The Platinum Tour: $25.25 for adults, $22.73 for seniors and students, $12.25 for children
Mansion Only: $16.25 for adults $14.63 for seniors and students $6.25 for children
Tour length: Varies, but if you're taking in the whole shebang I recommend that you allow three hours, which will allow for ample souvenir shopping time. Restaurants on-site.

What can I say? It's the home of the "King of Rock'n'Roll" — and so much more. Even non-Elvis fans should see this American landmark for its significance in pop-culture history alone. I am of the Beatles generation and am ashamed to admit that I did not give Elvis the credit he deserved until I re-examined him after a Graceland tour. (I've seen Graceland so many times now that I have lost count.) I insist that all of my out-of-town guests (and other Memphians) pay Graceland a visit, and I have yet to know a single person who did not come away glad they went.

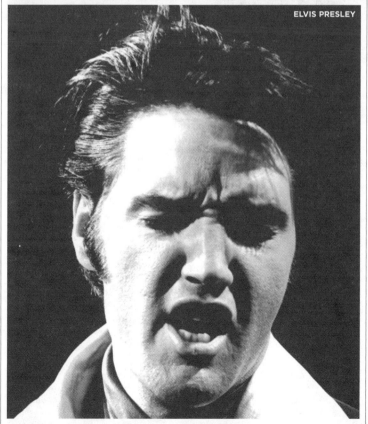

ELVIS PRESLEY

ELVIS PRESLEY: 68 COMEBACK SPECIAL

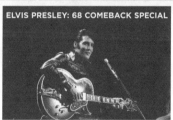

It's an extremely well-organized tour, complete with audio guides featuring the voices of Elvis and Priscilla themselves.

Choose between a tour of the mansion only, or purchase the Platinum Tour, which includes the mansion and Meditation Garden, the car museum (my personal favorite), Elvis' custom jets (pretty amazing), and the Sincerely Elvis exhibit. There is also a choice of casual dining spots and lots of shopping opportunities. Hey, buying Elvis souvenirs is practically required when visiting Memphis!

Interesting note: The fastest-growing segment of Graceland visitors each year is the under-35 crowd, most of whom were not even born when he was a fixture on the airwaves and the screen.

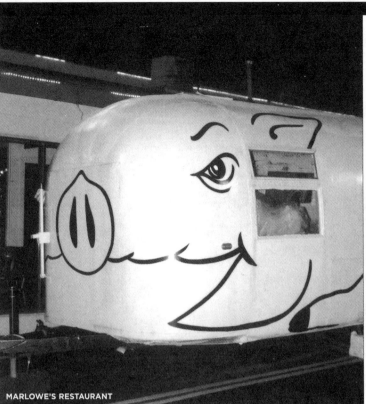

There are two eateries across the street from the mansion, nestled among the plaza's many shops and museums. Rockabilly's Diner is open from 8:30 a.m. until 5:30 p.m., offering breakfast, lunch, snacks, and early supper. The Chrome Grille is open from 11 a.m. until 6 p.m., offering luncheon fare, snacks, and early supper. You're also invited to enjoy the Shake, Split, & Dip Ice Cream Parlor (open during the warm months). All options offer an air-conditioned respite from the summer heat, not to mention a chance to get off of your feet.

Kid-Friendly Hotels

$	-	$40-$59
$$	-	$60-$89
$$$	-	$90-189
$$$$	-	$190+

Like many airport areas, South Memphis is a mixed bag. You'll find some well-known chains with clean and reputable properties (that cater mostly to the business traveler) and some substandard properties. A number of the hotels along I-55 and on Democrat Road are both convenient and comfortable. There are two hotels that I can recommend with confidence:

Elvis Presley's
Heartbreak Hotel - $$
3677 Elvis Presley Boulevard
332-1000, 877-777-0606
www.heartbreakhotel.net

Heart-shaped, outdoor, unheated swimming pool and a fitness center. 1950s kitsch, right across the street from Graceland. Features free Elvis movies and free continental breakfast.

Holiday Inn Select - $$
2240 Democrat Road
332-1130, 888-444-7789

This full-service hotel features an outdoor, unheated pool, fitness center, and restaurant with room service. It's just minutes from Graceland and close to I-240 for easy access to the rest of the city.

Touliatos Nature Center
2020 Brooks Road
346-8065
www.waterplants.net

Just west of the airport, nestled in a concrete jungle of industrial parks and fast-food joints, lies a 20-acre nature center, complete with woodlands, wetlands, and a meadow. Plato Touliatos established Touliatos Nature Center in 2003 on the grounds of his 40-year-old nursery. In recognition of his efforts, the state of Tennessee designated it as the city's third arboretum (the Carlisle S. Page Arboretum within Historic Elmwood Cemetery and the Old Forest Arboretum of Overton Park are the other two). Take the kids down the trails of this living classroom and you'll discover more than 40 species of birds and wildlife, or connect with a naturalist for some hands-on learning. The center also offers various seminars throughout the year, some of which are geared toward kids.

Kid-Friendly Restaurants
There are a number of restaurants in this area, but the only ones I'd recommend are listed below.

$	-	$1 - $9
$$	-	$10 - $19
$$$	-	$20+

Marlowe's Restaurant - $ - $$
4381 Elvis Presley Boulevard
332-4159

Lunch & dinner. Just a few blocks south of Graceland, this place hits the spot with BBQ, sandwiches, and blue-plate specials. They provide friendly service in a setting filled with memorabilia. Look for the hot-pink trailer parked outside the eatery. The colorful contraption is painted to look like a pig and it's hard to miss.

Graceland - $
3734 Elvis Presley Boulevard
332-3322, 800-238-2000
www.elvis.com

CHAPTER 6

Neighboring Cities of Shelby County

Smaller communities offer attractions of their own

S.Y. WILSON AND COMPANY, INC.

MOST OF THE TOWNS and communities listed in this chapter are independent townships with their own political leadership, but physically, their boundaries are shared with Memphis. Folks can drive from Memphis to Germantown to Collierville, for example, and never realize they have traveled from one town to another. All are an easy distance from Memphis. A drive from the downtown Welcome Center to the Arlington Visitor Center, 28 miles to the east, for example, only takes about 30 to 35 minutes, depending on traffic.

Arlington

Arlington Chamber of Commerce
867-2620
www.townofarlington.org

Situated at the eastern-most edge of Shelby County, north of Interstate-40, this community was first incorporated as Haysville in 1878, and then changed its name to Arlington in 1883. For years, it was a rural expanse of farmland, but in recent decades, it has attracted a number of major businesses and developments, including a $1.5

million recreational complex.

From a tourist's perspective, Arlington's appeal is most evident at its picturesque center. Its small-town charm is complemented by vintage homes dating back to the 1870s and by the 106-year-old country store, S.Y. Wilson and Company, Inc. Every spring, hundreds of people attend Arlington in April, a celebration of the town featuring walking tours, crafts, a Civil War re-enactment, and a car show.

In addition to Arlington's historic attractions, it is also the site of the new Memphis/Shelby County Welcome Center, on the south side of I-55.

Sites and Attractions

S.Y. Wilson and Company, Inc.
12020 Walker Street
867-2226
www.sywilson.com
Open Monday – Saturday:
8 a.m. – 6 p.m. (spring & summer)
8 a.m. – 5 p.m. (fall & winter)
I love this kind of place! Four generations of the Wilson family have run this general merchandise and hardware store since 1893. Go back in time as you browse through this landmark, and see what treasures you can find. In addition to the expected hardware goods, you'll find seasonal gifts, crafts, and gardening items. I could spend a solid hour here – or more.

Memphis/Shelby County Welcome Center
I-55 at the Arlington Exit
543-5333
www.memphistravel.com
Open 7 days a week:
9 a.m. - 5 p.m. – November-March
9 a.m. - 6 p.m. – April-October
Closed Thanksgiving Day, Christmas Day, New Year's Day
Gift shop on-site
Find out all you need to know about visiting the communities of Shelby County. Counselors are on duty to answer your questions, and there are plenty of brochures to browse through. There's also a gift shop on-site.

Kid-Friendly Restaurants
$ - $1 - $9
$$ - $10 - $19
$$$ - $20+

Vinegar Jim's - $
12062 Forrest Street
867-7568
Lunch & dinner. Closed Sunday. Southern-style family fare. Meat'n' veggies, desserts.

BARTLETT PERFORMING ARTS AND CONFERENCE CENTER

Bartlett

Chamber of Commerce
372-9457
www.cityofbartlett.org
Located 11 miles northeast of downtown Memphis, Bartlett is accessible via Highways 64, 70, and I-40. The town was founded in 1829 as a stop on the stagecoach line that ran between Memphis and Nashville. In the 1850s, it became a station on the Memphis and Ohio Railroad and was known as Union Depot. The town was incorporated in 1866 and renamed Bartlett after Major Gabriel M. Bartlett, a merchant and planter who owned a large plantation along Stage Road.

Today, Bartlett is home to 40,000 residents. It is also home to 18 public parks, a golf course, community center, and state-of-the-art recreational and fitness center.

Sites and Attractions

Bartlett Performing Arts and Conference Center
3663 Appling Road
385-6440
www.bpacc.org
Call for events, show-times and prices.

This facility attracts world-renowned performers and major touring shows, and it hosts local events – all of which are suitable for children.

Bartlett Museum in the Historic Gotten House
2969 Court Street
373-8433
www.cityofbartlett.org
Open 1st and 3rd Sunday of each month, 2 – 4 p.m. or by appointment
Price: Free
Tour length: 30 minutes
Operated by the Bartlett Historical Society, this New England saltbox-style home was built in 1871 and remained in the Gotten family until 1948. Displays include historical files and photographs, period furniture and artifacts, all serving to illustrate Bartlett's colorful history.

For the past several years, the Bartlett Historical Society has sponsored a historical presentation and costumed walking tour that centers on the Bartlett-Ellendale Cemetery and Fullview Church Cemetery. Ancestors "come alive" to tell their stories, and the 51st Tennessee Confederate Infantry presents a Civil War encampment. Call the museum for dates.

Davies Manor Plantation
9336 Davies Plantation Road
386-0715
www.daviesmanorplantation.org
Open April – December 22
Tuesday – Saturday: noon – 4 p.m.
Last tour begins at 3:30 p.m.
Price: $5 for adults, $3 for students, preschoolers free
Tour length: 30-45 minutes

Yes, this is in East Memphis, but it's way, way east in an area also known as Brunswick. It's not that hard to find, though, and if you're a history buff, it's worth the trip.

This is not a Tara-style plantation home, though the long gravel drive gives you that initial feeling. The Davies Manor Plantation is Shelby County's oldest furnished log-and-chink home that is open for tours. Built around 1830, this frontier home remained in the Davies family for more than 100 years. Davies Plantation is a reminder that just a few decades before the Civil War,

most of this country was a wilderness. The house and its furnishings are simple, even crude. The wood smells old — in a good way. The plantation is listed on the National Historic Register.

Kid-Friendly Restaurants
$ - $1 - $9
$$ - $10 - $19
$$$ - $20+

Coletta's - $$
2850 Appling Road
383-1122
Lunch & dinner. Closed for lunch on Sunday. A mainstay on

GRIDLEY'S BBQ

Memphis' Italian cuisine scene for years with lasagna, ravioli, and pizza. One of two Memphis-area locations.

Dixie Café - $-$
2861 Bartlett Boulevard
377-2211
Lunch & dinner. Homestyle, Southern cooking with generous portions. Hot rolls and great desserts. One of two Memphis-area locations.

Gridley's BBQ - $-$$
6842 Stage Road
377-8055
Lunch & dinner. One of Memphis's pioneer BBQ eateries and still one of the best. Remember: If it's Memphis BBQ, it's pork. One of six Memphis-area locations.

Pig-N-Whistle - $-$$
2740 Bartlett Road
386-3300

PIG-N-WHISTLE

Lunch & dinner. Delicious BBQ in a casual, comfortable atmosphere. One of three Memphis-area locations.

Side Porch Steak House - $$-$$$
5689 Stage Road
377-2484
Dinner. The name says it all: steak and all the trimmings, plus other Southern specialties.

Annual Events

Summertime Concert Series in Freeman Park
Sundays at 5 p.m., June-August
385-5589
dmorrison@cityofbartlett.org

Bartlett Celebration (October)
385-5589

Collierville

Chamber of Commerce
853-1949
www.colliervillechamber.com
Collierville is just 25 miles east of downtown Memphis on Highway 72/Poplar Avenue. Its early settlements date between 1819-1824, with the town of Collierville established in the mid-1830s. A surveyor's error placed Collierville in Mississippi until 1838. It was incorporated in 1850, but the small town burned to the ground during the Civil War.

In 1870, Collierville re-incorporated, and the Town Square was established. An estimated 43,000 people live there now, and it's growing fast (one of the fastest-growing cities in the country, as a matter of fact).

Annual events include the Sunset on the Square concert series, the Christmas Parade, and Christmas in Collierville.

Sites and Attractions

Historic Town Square
The heart of the city, this classic town square is lined with more than 50 antique shops, crafts and gift shops, art galleries, eateries, and other businesses. There are several restaurants as well. You could spend hours here – not to mention more than a few dollars.

In addition to the shopping, dining and general browsing, there is a log cabin on-site that was used as a stagecoach stop in the mid-1800s.

SIDE PORCH STEAK HOUSE

SILVER CABOOSE RESTAURANT AND SODA FOUNTAIN

You'll also see the train depot. Nearby is the Savannah, an executive rail car built in 1915, a caboose, and an old steam engine, which was built in 1912. Have you met a child yet who wasn't intrigued by trains?

Biblical Resource Center and Museum
140 East Mulberry
854-9578
www.biblical-museum.org
Monday – Friday: 9 a.m.-5 p.m.
Call for price.
Tour length: 1 hour
In the heart of historic Collierville, the Biblical Resource Center and Museum is truly a one-of-a-kind experience designed with young people in mind. The goal is to enhance the stories of the Bible through tangible, visual displays. It also provides materials for teachers and scholars. Replicas of Hebrew and Christian artifacts of the Middle East and Europe are on view such as: a panel from the Black Obelisk of Shalmaneser III, a full-size copy of the Rosetta Stone, and other hands-on exhibits. There is a multimedia library with information on Mediterranean, Egyptian, Near Eastern, and Palestinian history of Hebrew and Christian scripture. A video presentation is available for groups of 15 or more. Museum store is on-site.

Harrell Performing Arts Theatre
440 Powell Road West
853-3228

www.colliervilleparks.org
Call for show times and prices.
Great family fare at way off-Broadway prices. This community theater attracts strong, local talent for surprisingly good productions – virtually all of which are appropriate for children.

Kid-Friendly Restaurants
$ - $1 - $9
$$ - $10 - $19
$$$ - $20+

Café Grill - $-$$
120 West Mulberry Street
853-7511
Lunch & dinner. Daily buffet. Chicken, hamburger steaks, veggies, potpies, and cobblers.

Corky's - $-$$
743 W. Poplar, 405-4999
Lunch & dinner. Acclaimed wet and dry BBQ. One of four Memphis-area locations.

Dinstuhl's Famous Candies – $
101 North Center Street
854-4474
Candy. Lots of candy. All kinds of candy. And probably the most delicious chocolate-covered strawberries in the whole world (available only when in season).

Huey's - $
2130 West Poplar
854-4455
Lunch & dinner. Just like its many other locations: juicy burgers, chicken fingers, soup, salads, etc. All patrons encouraged to shoot toothpicks into the ceiling and to write on the walls.

Silver Caboose Restaurant and Soda Fountain - $
132 East Mulberry Street
853-0010
Lunch seven days a week. This delightful eatery is a real family pleaser with Southern hot-plate lunches, salads, homemade pies, and frozen pecan balls.

FEDEX ST. JUDE CLASSIC GOLF TOURNAMENT

Annual Events
listed on www.collierville.com

Fair on the Square
1st weekend in May
853-6228

Christmas in Collierville
December
853-1949

Sunset on the Square
Summer Concert Series
June & July
Thursdays at 7:00 p.m.
427-5457

Germantown

Chamber of Commerce
755-1200
www.germantownchamber.com
Sharing city limits with Memphis, Germantown enjoys a reputation as an upscale community with fine homes and great shopping. It was first organized as the village of Pea Ridge in 1833 and renamed Germantown in 1836 and chartered in 1841. The town suffered major setbacks during the Civil War and the yellow fever epidemics, and it remained a small town well into the late 1960s. Now Germantown has a population of roughly 40,000.

More than 700 acres of parkland place a city park within one-half mile of every resident. A 75-acre nature center is under development along the Wolf River.

The Germantown Performing Arts Centre is a facility of superior design with near-perfect acoustics. It is home to a symphony orchestra, chorus, and community theater and attracts some of the world's most famous performers and touring companies.

Known as "horse country," especially for English-style equestrians, the city is well known as host of the annual Germantown Charity Horse Show. It also welcomes the FedEx St. Jude Classic golf tournament, a highly-anticipated stop on the PGA tour. For dates, go to www.pga.com.

Sites and Attractions

Germantown Performing Arts Centre (GPAC)
1801 Exeter Road
751-7500
www.gpacweb.com
Call for prices, performance schedule and show times.
GPAC is an attractive, contemporary facility that presents world-class touring companies and local performing arts. My husband Sledge and I took Will and a friend to see the Chinese Acrobats when the show was in town. We bought our tickets just a few days beforehand and ended up on the back row. No problem! We could see perfectly. There's not a bad seat in the house!

Kid-Friendly Restaurants

$ - $1 - $9
$$ - $10 - $19
$$$ - $20+

Belmont Grill - $
9102 Poplar Pike
624-6001
Lunch & dinner. BBQ, ribs, steak burgers, and shrimp. It can get crowded, especially at suppertime.

Germantown Commissary - $-$$
2290 South Germantown
754-5540
Lunch & dinner. A longtime local favorite for BBQ lovers. In addition to BBQ sandwiches, it specializes in BBQ nachos and shrimp.

Three Oaks Grill - $$
2285 South Germantown Road
757-8225
Lunch & dinner. Handsome setting. Very popular. Delicious food: fresh seafood, steaks, grilled trout, and chicken dishes.

West Street Diner – $
2076 West Street
757-2191
Breakfast, lunch & dinner. Country cooking. Casual and tasty.

The Bottom Line – $
1817 Kirby Parkway
755-2481
Lunch & dinner. Open until midnight weekdays, 1:00 a.m. on weekends. A "Cheers bar" atmosphere. Burgers, salads, and sandwiches plus prime rib, plate lunches, and delicious homemade specialties.

Annual Events

Hunter Jumper Horse Shows
May
756-6347

Germantown Charity Horse Show
June
754-0009
www.gchs.org

Germantown Fall Festival
September
757-9212
www.germantownchamber.com

Fourth of July Family Celebration
July
755-1200

Lakeland

Chamber of Commerce
382-5027
www.cityoflakeland.com
Lakeland is situated just 12 miles east of Memphis, off I-40. It has an interesting history. The town was originally founded in the 1960s as an amusement park called Lakeland Playland. It had a 275-acre lake, suspended cable cars, miniature roller coaster, and life-sized fiberglass dinosaurs. When the park was closed, its founder subdivided the land into residential lots on which some of the area's most beautiful homes are now located.

Lakeland was incorporated in 1977 and now bosts more than 6,000 residents. It remains a residential community with only one real "attraction," the Belz Factory Outlet World.

Sites and Attractions

Lakeland Factory Outlet Mall
3536 Canada Road
386-3180
Monday – Saturday: 10 a.m. – 9 p.m.
Sunday: 1 - 6 p.m.
Smaller than many factory outlet malls I've seen around the country, this facility still offers some everyday bargains, often up to 75 percent off. Stores include Bass Company Store, Dress Barn, Nike, Casual Male – Big & Tall, Vitamin World, Old Time Pottery, Hushpuppies, and others.

Annual Events

Fourth of July Fireworks
382-5027

Christmas Parade
382-5027

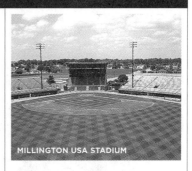
MILLINGTON USA STADIUM

Millington, Tennessee

Chamber of Commerce
872-1486
www.millingtonchamber.com
In the late 1870s, the communities of Millwood and Glencoe formed a new town called Millington (named after plantation owners Mr. and Mrs. George Millington), where a railroad station was built on the Chesapeake and Ohio Railroad line. Millington was incorporated in 1903.

Once home to the huge Millington Naval Station, the "Navy in the Heartland," the facility is now headquarters for Naval Support Activity Mid-South with the Navy's Bureau of Personnel as its primary tenant. In addition to its many, major economic initiatives, Milling-ton offers a surprising array of family-centered activities.

The U.S. Olympic Baseball Team is based here. Fans can watch the American team take on international competition throughout the summer. The USA Baseball Stadium also hosts the National Junior College World Series. The adjacent state-of-the-art Rodeo Arena is the site of IPRA-sanctioned competitions.

Also in and around Millington, Eagle Lake Refuge, Meeman-Shelby State Park, and Shelby Forest all offer hiking, bird watching, and other outdoor recreational activities.

∞ MILLINGTON TIDBIT
Millington's most famous native? Justin Timberlake

BELLE AIRE BIPLANE RIDES

for that the day we took off. We also received a videotape keepsake of our afternoon.

I was told that their youngest riders were 3 years old, but their parents were serious aviation buffs. Personally, I'd recommend this for children at least 5 or 6 years old.

Harris Produce Farms
7521 Sledge Road (off Austin Peay)
872-0696
June (call for dates)
Tuesday – Friday: 8 a.m. – 6 p.m.
Saturday: 8 a.m. – 2 p.m.
Price: $2.25 to pick your own quart
or $4.50 per pre-picked quart
Summertime and the pickin' is easy. Now this is something the kids don't get to do every day – especially city kids. Let them gather their own blueberries. The whole family is invited to participate, or you can let someone else pick them for you, but it costs more, and where's the fun in that?

Jones Orchard
Two Millington locations:
7170 Highway 51 North
873-3150
6850 Singleton Parkway
872-0703
www.jonesorchard.com
June (call for dates)
Monday – Saturday: 8 a.m. – 6 p.m.
Sunday: Noon – 6 p.m.
40 cents a pound if you pick, $13 for a bushel if they pick (other price-pick options are also available). After you and the kids pluck your vegetables at Harris Farms, run on over to Jones Orchard for your pick of the fruit.

Memphis Motorsports Park
5500 Taylor Forge Drive
358-7223
www.memphismotorsportspark.com
March – September. Call or go online for schedules and prices. Gift shop on-site, concessions during events.
Exciting. And *loud*. The Memphis Motorsports Park hosts

Sites and Attractions

Belle Aire Biplane Rides
Charles Baker Airport
3870 Fite Rd.
481-1935
www.belleaireaviation.com
April – October: 8 a.m. - dark
Price: begins at $99 per ten-minute ride (for up to two passengers) or $179/30 min. Reservations required.
Tour length: 30 minutes
Wow! This is so cool. We took the whole family for a total of three rides one Sunday afternoon. It is really a thrilling, memorable family outing that we all loved. We soared between 80 and 100 m.p.h. to a maximum of 1,500 feet. If you love a feeling of total freedom and a look at our earthly world from a fresh perspective, this is the experience for you and the kids.

Belle Aire offers fantastic aerial sightseeing rides aboard a 1930s-style biplane – and you haven't seen the Mississippi River or downtown Memphis until you've seen it from above. The flight is high enough for a spectacular view and low enough to see just distant details. In cooler months, you are given barnstormer-style headgear to wear, but it was a little too warm

MEMPHIS MOTORSPORTS PARK

action-packed auto and other motor sports, amateur and professional, at four different tracks covering 600 acres. This is also home to the NASCAR Busch Series, the NASCAR Truck Series, and the NHRA Powerade Drag Racing Series. There are weekly races and lots of special events. Check out the Race On Driving Experience, where dad (or mom) can do ride-alongs. Ride-alongs are $100/6 laps, solo drives are $275/10 laps, $399/20 laps. (866) 472-2366.

Millington USA Stadium
4351 Babe Howard Boulevard
872-8326
www.usabaseballstadium.org
Call or check the website for a list of events and schedules.
A superb multipurpose facility, the USA Stadium is the home field for the American Olympic Baseball team. Teams from all over the world (more than 18 countries) have played here. Other baseball championships and World Series are played here in tournaments that run from February through August.

The stadium also hosts a number of rodeos from spring through autumn. The famous Goat Days Festival is held here, as is a Native-American powwow. In other words, great baseball is just the beginning.

Old Millington Vineyard & Winery
6748 Old Millington Road
873-4114
www.tennesseewines.com
www.allamericanwineries.com
The Old Millington Vineyard and Winery was established in 1995 and opened to the public in 2000. It produces a selection of grape and fruit wines. While it may not compete in size and scope with its California or New York "cousins," the winery can offer you and the kids a solid introduction to the growing and harvesting of grapes and an interesting lesson in Winemaking 101. What's more, the staff is really, really nice.

Kid-Friendly Restaurants
$ - $1 - $9
$$ - $10 - $19
$$$ - $20+

Old Timer's Restaurant - $
7918 C Street
872-6464
Breakfast (on weekends), lunch, & dinner. This place is very popular with the locals. They offer friendly, down-home service and tasty, Southern-style food.

Miss Sipps Catfish Saloon - $-$$
7838 Church Street
873-4746
Lunch & dinner. This "catfish saloon" offers everything from sandwiches and other casual fare to steaks. Carry-out and take-out are also available.

Mamma Mannellos - $-$$
7936 US Highway 51 North
873-0200
Lunch & dinner. Mamma Mannellos serves tasty, dependable Italian fare with something on the menu to please virtually any age. It's a great choice for picky eaters.

Annual Events

IPRA National Championship Rodeo
June & July
872-8326

NASCAR Craftsman Truck Series at Memphis Motorsports Park
June
866-40-SPEED
www.memphismotorsportspark.com

International Goat Days at USA Stadium
September
872-4559
www.internationalgoatdays.com

NASCAR Busch Series & the NHRA O'Reilly Mid-South Nationals at Memphis Motorsports Park
October
866-40-SPEED
www.memphismotorsportspark.com

INTERNATIONAL GOAT DAYS

CHAPTER 7

Regional Highlights (within 100 miles)

There's another world beyond the city limits

FLY FISHING IN ARKANSAS

MY HUSBAND SLEDGE and I love to drive the back roads. We enjoy the process of getting there. We stop when we feel like it, explore the country stores, tour caves, or hike nearly forgotten trails. We enjoy the modest, small-town museums, many of which are located in the post office or occasionally someone's home.

There are many such experiences to be found in the three states that surround Shelby County. There are places that make for great day trips while others are worth an overnight stay.

One thing is for sure, there are too many regional attractions to list in this chapter (that could be a book itself!), so I've selected a few that might arouse your interest.

Arkansas

General Information:
www.arkansas.com
www.accessarkansas.org
www.arkansaskids.com

Arkansas State Parks:
www.ArkansasStateParks.com

Arkansas Highway Map and Vacation Information:
1-800-NATURAL or
www.arkansashighways.com

Arkansas Game and Fish Information:
501-223-6300

Arkansas is currently undergoing an ambitious upgrade of its interstate highway system. You might want to get an update on construction activities before setting out by calling 501-569-2227 or logging onto: www.ArkansasInterstates.com.

LOUISIANA PURCHASE STATE PARK

as Crawley's Ridge, the Arkansas Delta, like the Mississippi Delta, parallels the Mississippi River flood plain. The land is flat, the soil is rich, and these factors make the area ideal for farming. Fields of cotton, wheat, corn, soybeans, peanuts, and rice are common sights, as are catfish farms. Like the Mississippi Delta, this region is well known for its music, especially blues and gospel.

In addition to Interstates 55 (heading north from Memphis) and 40 (heading west) and the usual highways and back roads, there are two scenic byways that are well worth your time: Crowley's Ridge Parkway and the Great River Road.

LOUISIANA PURCHASE STATE PARK

Blackton
(Roughly 90 miles - halfway between Brinkley and Helena)

Louisiana Purchase State Park Highway
362 off U.S. 49
1-888-AT PARKS
www.historystateparks.com
Open 7 days a week: dawn until 10 p.m.

They don't call Arkansas "The Natural State" for nothing. It's teeming with state parks, forests, and outdoor recreation areas. I've listed a couple of the better-known parks, but you might want to log onto the state park website, listed below, if you want a bigger picture. Arkansas is divided into six regions: the Ozarks, River Valley, Ouachitas, Central, Timberlands, and the Delta. Staying within 100 miles of Memphis, I've focused exclusively on the Delta region.

The Delta Region

In 1541, Hernando de Soto first crossed the Mississippi River into what is now known as the Delta region of Arkansas. (Parkin State Archeological State Park includes an ancient village, which may have been one of de Soto's stops as he moved west.) In 1803, the Louisiana Purchase added the Arkansas territories as a new frontier for a growing America.

With the exception of the 200-mile stretch of "highlands" known

A 900-foot boardwalk takes you over the swamps to a monument marking the starting point of the surveys for the 1803 Louisiana Purchase. Interpretative panels instruct along the way, explaining the history of the purchase. It's a nature trail with history tossed in, or maybe a history lesson with nature tossed in. My husband and I love this kind of stuff. The kids like running ahead, hoping to spot critters.

Blytheville
(64 miles from Memphis)

Blytheville Heritage Museum
210 W. Main Street
870-763-2525
http://blytheville.dina.org/community/sights.html
Monday – Friday:
9:30 a.m. – 5 p.m.

Frankly, I drive to Blytheville for the bookstore alone (see below), but while you're in town, learn a lot about the history and pioneers of the area's cotton and logging industries at this heritage museum. There is also a pictorial tribute to Eaker Air Force Base, which was once the lifeblood of the town. According to Mary Gay Shipley, owner of That Bookstore in Blytheville, this little gem of a museum is "about to be even better." The city and the Department of Transportation are providing funds to restore two historic landmarks, such as the bus depot, to accommodate expanded exhibits.

Lights of the Delta
Blytheville Air Force Base
www.lightsofthedelta.com
Mid November – End of December
Seven days a week

You have to see it to believe it. People drive for miles to take in roughly 40 acres of magnificent lights — some abstract, some of specific scenes, most in motion. You can travel by car (with your headlights turned off) or better yet, take it all in by horse-drawn carriage. This is worth the trip, and your kids will love it. This festival is ranked as one of the top 100 festivals in North America by the American Bus Association.

That Bookstore in Blytheville
316 West Main Street
870-763-3333
www.tbib.com
Monday – Saturday:
9:30 a.m. – 6 p.m.
Open Sundays: 1 – 5 p.m., except from July 4 through Labor Day

This charming old bookstore has a friendly staff. It's no wonder the likes of John Grisham and Ferrol Sams prefer to do book signings here. A landmark of the community's Main Street U.S.A. program, That Bookstore is *the* bookstore. Storeowner Mary Gay Shipley is not only a knowledgeable and helpful bookseller, she's a great promoter for the city.

Crowley's Ridge State Park
Runs roughly from 80 miles north (Paragould) to 80 miles south of Memphis (Helena). Cabins and camping are southwest of Paragould.
870-573-6751
Cabin reservations
800-264-2405
www.ArkansasStateParks.com
Open 7 days a week: 8 a.m. – 5 p.m.

Crowley's Ridge is named for Benjamin Crowley, who moved here in the 1800s after his land was flooded by the New Madrid

CROWLEY'S RIDGE STATE PARK

earthquake. This is the Delta's only "highlands," and features a 200-mile route across the top of the ridge that passes near five state parks, museums, lakes, Civil War sites, and more. You'll find cabins, camping, boating, fishing, nature trail, picnic area, and a restaurant.

HELENA

Helena/West Helena
(75 miles from Memphis)

Blues Corner
105 Cherry Street/Historic District
870-338-3501
www.arkansas.com/attractions
Monday – Saturday: 9 a.m. – 5 p.m.
After Christmas: Sundays: 1 – 5 p.m.

Blues fans will want to check out their collection of records, CDs, tapes, books, and memorabilia.

Delta Cultural Center
Missouri and Natchez Street/
Cherry Street Historic District
870-338-4350, 800-358-0972
www.deltaculturalcenter.com
Monday – Saturday: 9 a.m. – 5 p.m.
Sunday: 1 – 5 p.m.

This museum is housed in several historic buildings in downtown Helena. The "Heritage of Determination" exhibit is in the restored 1912 train depot, and the "Delta Sounds" exhibit occupies two renovated stores in the Visitors Center. The history of the Arkansas Delta is covered extensively, from the earliest Native American inhabitants to Spanish and French explorers, planters, slaves, sharecroppers, river pilots, trappers, and many more. It's a multi-media facility that includes "The Great Boat Race," an activity geared toward kids. The region's blues and gospel music heritage is also presented at this major attraction and is a "must" for visitors.

Delta Heritage Tours
118 Waverly Wood
800-338-8972
Select a customized tour:
Sights and Sounds and Tastes of the Delta
Juke Joint Tour
Historical Homes
Gospel and Blues
Call ahead for reservations.

DELTA CULTURAL CENTER

ARKANSAS STATE UNIVERSITY MUSEUM

I'm a blues fan, so this kind of thing appeals to me. Delta Heritage provides a cultural and musical tour of Helena that includes a gospel church service, a live performance of America's longest-running blues radio show (*King Biscuit Hour*), and a visit to the Delta Cultural Center. With advance notice, you can schedule a customized tour that includes historic homes and a crawfish farm, and even get a home-cooked meal.

Phillips County Museum
623 Pecan Street
870-338-7790

Offering a history of Helena and its role as a major river port, you'll find Native-American and Civil War artifacts, as well as period paintings of Helena's seven Civil War generals. Established in 1929.

Pillow-Thompson House
Perry and Beech Streets
870-338-8535
www.pccua.edu/pillowthompson

Open Wednesday – Saturday:
10 a.m. – 4 p.m.
Lunch served first Thursday of the month, reservations required

Built in 1896, this is a lovely example of Queen Anne architecture, an authentically furnished Victorian home full of Southern history. While it is the only Helena home open to the public year-round, it is just one of many beautiful, historic homes that are worth seeing as part of a memorable and relaxing drive around town.

Jonesboro
(65 miles from Memphis)

African-American Cultural Center
613 Fisher Street
870-932-6013
Call ahead for an appointment.

With a focus on the history of Craighead County, this museum covers the arrival of the first slave in 1860 to present day.

Arkansas State University Museum
110 Cooley Drive
870-972-2074
http://museum.astate.edu
Monday – Friday: 9 a.m.-4 p.m.
Saturday and Sunday: 1-5 p.m.
Free admission, but $2 per person donation recommended

Opened in 1936 with a single case of artifacts, this pioneer museum has expanded dramatically to include a turn-of-the-century village, along with Native-American exhibits and artifacts. There are plenty of fossils and real mastodon bones and exhibits.

Lepanto
(Roughly 50 miles from Memphis)

Museum Lepanto USA
Main Street
870-475-2384, 870-475-2591
Summer only – Wednesday and Friday: 1 – 4 p.m.
Free, but donations accepted

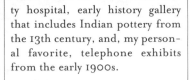

If you saw the TV movie *A Painted House*, based on the John Grisham book, then you might recognize this place. Replicas of old-time stores are furnished with original merchandise that illustrate the history of the Delta. Older kids might enjoy recognizing familiar products in old-time packaging. There are also displays commemorating the Civil War, World War II, and the Vietnam War.

Marianna
(50 miles from Memphis)

Marianna/Lee County Museum
67 West Main Street
870-295-2469
Open by appointment only

This museum features a number of exhibits, including a general store, a parlor, and kitchen, with an overview of cotton farming. There are also displays on the Civil War and World War II. Unfortunately, the museum is not handicapped accessible.

St. Francis National Forest
Arkansas 44, east of Marianna
870-295-5278
www.fs.fed.us

Just outside of Marianna is the 21,000-acre St. Francis National Forest. You'll find the usual outdoor recreational opportunities, plus a scenic byway that runs right through the woods.

Marked Tree
(35 miles from Memphis)

Marked Tree Delta Area Museum
308 Frisco Street
870-358-4998
Monday – Friday: noon - 5 p.m.
Saturday: 8 a.m. – noon
Free, but donations accepted

Guests enter this museum through a façade of a 19th-century general store to discover a replica of a small-town communi-

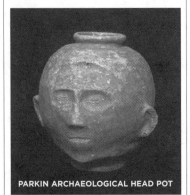

PARKIN ARCHAEOLOGICAL HEAD POT

ty hospital, early history gallery that includes Indian pottery from the 13th century, and, my personal favorite, telephone exhibits from the early 1900s.

Parkin
(roughly 30 miles from Memphis)

Parkin Archaeological State Park
Jct. of U.S. 64 and Ark. 184
870-755-2500
www.ArkansasStateParks.com
Tuesday – Saturday: 8 a.m. – 5 p.m.
Sunday: noon to 5 p.m.
Closed Monday
Price: $2.75 for adults, $1.75 for children 6-12, under 5, free

Overlooking the St. Francis River on the preserved site of a 17-acre Native-American village from the Mississippian Period (1000-1550 A.D.), this state park includes a research station, museum, interpretive center, and periodic digs and demonstrations. Parkin offers an interesting diversion for locals as well as tourists who enjoy the fishing, nature trails, and gift shop. There are also cabin rentals nearby. Most kids are well entertained here. Living History Days offers added fun and interest in early October.

Piggott
(115 miles from Memphis)

Hemingway-Pfeiffer Museum and Educational Center
1021 W. Cherry Street
870-598-3487
http://hemingway.astate.edu
Monday – Friday: Guided tours hourly from 9:15 a.m. – 2:15 p.m.
Saturday: Guided tours at 12:15, 1:15, and 2:15 p.m. only
Reservations required.

Yes, this is beyond 100 miles of Memphis, but not by much, and how often do you get to see the home of one of America's greatest writers? It was here that Ernest Hemingway wrote *A Farewell to Arms*. Exhibits and memorabilia reflect his life and his marriage to wife Pauline.

PARKIN ARCHAEOLOGICAL STATE PARK

MUSEUM OF THE ARKANSAS GRAND PRAIRIE

Formerly the Stuttgart Agricultural Museum, this facility tells the story of the German settlers who gave the town its name and of its emergence as the nation's leading producer of rice. It sits on a 500,000-acre tall-grass prairie and features exhibits on pioneer life with authentic and re-created prairie structures, farm equipment, and duck hunting, for which Stuttgart is famous.

VILLAGE CREEK STATE PARK

St. Francis
(123 miles from Memphis)

Pumpkin Hollow
County Highway 341, just west of town
870-598-3568
www.pumpkinhollow.com
2nd location: Highway 264 and Bellview Road at Lowell, Arkansas (Same contact information)
*About 20 minutes from Kennett, MO
Late September – early November for Pumpkin Hollow
October only for the Forest of Fright (Call ahead for actual dates)
Days vary, but open 7 days a week near Halloween
Various price packages and activities available – call ahead to plan your particular visit.

Okay, so this is another eight miles past Piggott. In fact, this town is barely outside of Missouri, but as long as you've treated yourself to Hemingway's house, it's worth another few miles to treat the kids to Pumpkin Hollow (assuming you are traveling in the fall). This is where you'll find Dalton Farms, home of the state's largest corn-field maze (open September and October) and a big pumpkin

MUSEUM OF THE ARKANSAS GRAND PRAIRIE

patch that you can pick through from late September until early November. There are also pony rides, puppet shows, pig races, panning for "gold," and train rides. Caters mostly to school field trips but all are welcome.

Stuttgart
(102 miles from Memphis)

Museum of the Arkansas Grand Prairie
4th at Park
870-673-7001
http://www.ar-net.com/sttg
Open Tuesday – Friday:
8 a.m. – 4 p.m.
Saturday: 10 a.m. – 4 p.m.
Free, but donations are appreciated

Village Creek
(roughly 35 miles from Memphis)

Village Creek State Park
Ark. 284 between Wynne and Forrest City
870-238-9406
Cabin rentals:
800-264-2467
www.ArkansasStateParks.com
Open year-round: dawn to dusk.

This is a great little getaway. Stop at the visitor center first to get a lay of the land, which covers 7,000 acres. There are two fishing lakes, plenty of cabins, numerous campgrounds, hiking trails, you name it. Interpretive programs help you explore Crowley's Ridge (see earlier listing). In other words, if you and your kids like the outdoors, Village Creek is just one of many state parks that you should thoroughly enjoy.

∞ **HELENA TIDBIT:**
The King Biscuit Blues Festival is terrific – and it's great for kids IN THE DAYTIME. After dark, it gets a bit rowdy.

mainst@arkansas.net
Lights of the Delta Festival
(mid-November-December):
www.lightsofthedelta.com

Helena
King Biscuit Blues Festival
(October) – at the famed Sonny Boy's Music Hall: 301 Cherry Street
870-338-3501 (music hall)
870-338-8798 (event)

Jonesboro
Rockin' on the Ridge
(September)
870-932-2279

Stuttgart
World Championship Duck Calling Contest and Wings Over the Prairies Festival (November)
870-673-1602

West Memphis
Annual Livin' on the Levee Lion's Club Rodeo (August)
870-732-7598
E-mail: schristian@citywm.com

Mississippi

General Info:
www.visitmississippi.org
Mississippi Highway Map & Vacation Information:
866-SEE-MISS
(733-6477)
Hunting & Fishing Licenses:
800-546-4868
www.mdwfp.com
Natchez Trace Parkway:
662-680-4025
www.nps.gov/natr
Mississippi Delta Tourism Information:
800-467-3582

West Memphis
(2-3 miles from Memphis)

Southland Greyhound Park
1550 North Ingram Blvd.
870-735-3670, 800-467-6182
www.southlandgreyhound.com
Open seven days a week, year-round
Hours: 11 a.m. – 1 a.m.
Free downstairs, $1 clubhouse level

With speeds up to 40 m.p.h., greyhounds are as graceful as they are speedy. Of course, the betting is for adults only. I have been to

the dog track several times and enjoyed good food and an entertaining evening.

Annual Events

Batesville
Annual White River Water Carnival (August)
870-793-2378
bacofc@ipa.net

Blytheville
Chickasaw Chili Cook-off
(October)
870-763-2525

Mississippi is divided into five major areas: the Hills, the Delta, the Capital/River region, the Pines, and the Coastal region. Trying to stay within 100 miles (though it's so tempting to go farther), I focus on two regions: the Hills and the Delta.

Hills Region

Mississippi is arguably the most underrated state in America. People love to make fun of it (though not as much as Arkansas), when, in fact, Mississippi is complex, diverse, and fascinating. It is rich in character and history. A lot of what makes this state appealing can be found here in the Hill Country. This is the home of raw blues (influenced by 18th-century military drum and fife music as well as by traditional African rhythms) and a plantation legacy. It is the home of some of the world's most sophisticated and erudite writers and artists. It is where people still enjoy sitting on wicker furniture on the front veranda, telling tales of their ancestors (often exaggerated), while international business quietly revolutionizes modern commerce. It's where you'll find an elderly black man driving a tractor

or pumping gas — right after a month-long tour of Europe performing before thousands of music fans. It's a place of contrast and deep pride and should not be underestimated or overlooked.

The Hill Region is found at the northernmost part of the state. In contrast to its flat neighbor, the Delta, it offers a scenic landscape of gentle, rolling hills and an abundance of forests. In both the Delta and the Hill Country, a drive in May and June offers a look at the beautiful magnolia trees in full bloom (the magnolia is the official state flower); a summer tour reveals a landscape covered in kudzu; and a trip in October presents a sprawl of "white gold," thousands of acres of cotton bolls that make the land appear snow covered. If you only have time to take in a couple of destinations in this area, I recommend Holly Springs and Oxford as "must-sees."

Attractions:

Como
(45 miles south of Memphis)

Como Courtyard Bed & Breakfast
235 Main Street
800-527-4274
www.comocourtyard.com

If you want a night away from the city, Como is the home of "Hill Country Blues," and attracts a surprising number of visitors for such a small town. The Como Courtyard is not only the community's finest accommodation, it is the only one — but what a treat. You have the whole place to yourself in a lovely, 100-year-old, New Orleans-style building that leads into an open-air, walled courtyard with a charming guesthouse on the other side. You can rent just the front building or both. Its spacious living quarters can sleep up to seven people. And there's an outdoor hot tub, too. Rock stars have stayed here as well as the locals who just want a quiet retreat. Kids like this place as much as grownups.
* While you're in town, take a drive down Sycamore Street to see Como's famous row of 19th-century homes.

Como Steak House - $$
201 Main Street
662-526-9529
Monday – Saturday: Dinner only

Just a walk up the street from the Como Courtyard, this steak house is an attraction in its own right. The steaks are so good (as are other entrees) and the atmosphere so comfortable, people drive from as far away as 75 miles just for dinner. It's not uncommon to see entire busloads of people driving in for a meal, and on a couple of recent occasions, diners have dropped in via helicopter! Be sure to get a Como Delight for dessert. Upstairs is the Oyster Blues Bar, which offers fresh oysters on the half-shell, oyster po' boys, tuna skewers, shrimp, plus deli-style favorites.

Blades of Grass Gift Shop
213 Main Street
662-526-1011

A little bit of serendipity, this charming gift shop is an unexpected surprise. In a town that doesn't

SOUTHLAND GREYHOUND PARK

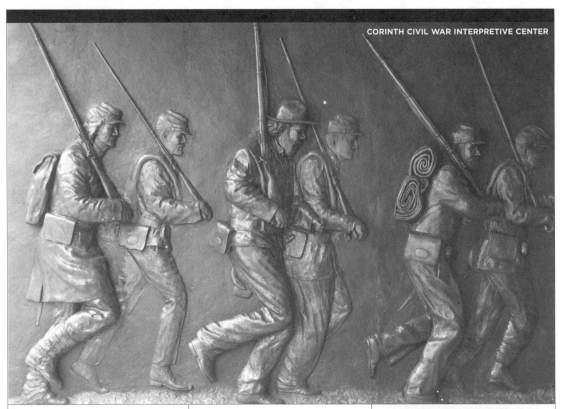

have a single streetlight, one can stroll Main Street and find this little gem between the Como Steak House and the Windy City Grille. It caters to the dining crowd, opening in the afternoon and welcoming customers until about 9 p.m. (closing sooner if it's a slow day). There's a terrific selection of silk and dried flowers, antiques, and original artworks — and most prices are surprisingly affordable. It's fun!

The Ranch - $$
223 Main Street
662-526-1000

Mosey on in for some great BBQ ribs, steaks, fried catfish — and according to my son Will — the best hamburgers anywhere. Located in an 18th-century former mercantile store complete with pressed-tin roof and hardwood floors, the décor is stylishly western, and the atmosphere is informal and comfortable. Be sure to try the chocolate cobbler!

Windy City Grille - $$
217 Main Street
662-526-0331
Tuesday – Saturday:
Lunch & dinner
Sunday: Lunch only

Como's newest attraction, the Windy City Grille is another reason people are willing to drive an hour or more to visit. Established by a family from Chicago, the restaurant is located in a restored, 19th-century building and offers freshly made, Chicago-style pizza and other specialties in a "Southern-fried" atmosphere. Special themed nights are a popular draw, and live blues rings out most Saturday nights.

Corinth
(93 miles from Memphis)
www.corinth.com

Battery Robinette
Linden Street
Open daily

Corinth is just south of the Tennessee state line and the Shiloh

BORROUM'S DRUG STORE

Military National Military Park. It was the site of fierce fighting during the Civil War because of its strategic location and its major railroads. There are a number of Civil War-related attractions here, including the Battery Robinette, which was constructed by the Federal Army and was a focal point of the bloody Battle of Corinth. The Corinth Civil War Interpretive Center gives visitors insight into this town's rich history.

Borroum's Drug Store
604 Waldron Street
662-286-6631
Monday – Saturday:
8:30 a.m. - 5 p.m.

This is the oldest family-operated drug store in the state. It opened in 1865. The pharmacist is fourth generation, and she's painted portraits of her predecessors, which are on display. Her son and daughter-in-law run the sundry. Light lunches are offered but most importantly, sodas are still made the old-fashioned way. You can also get root beer floats, banana splits, and other "classic" yummies. Just a grab a seat and sit a spell.

**Corinth Civil War
Interpretive Center**
301 Childs St.
662-287-9501
Summer: Monday – Saturday:
9 a.m.–5 p.m.
Sunday: 1-5 p.m.
Winter: Monday – Saturday:
9 a.m. – 4 p.m.
Sunday: 1 – 4 p.m.
Free

To get a proper perspective on the Civil War battles of this region, it's worth a trip to this impressive interpretive center on the grounds of the historic Battery Robinette. This is an exceptionally well-

designed facility, which presents a detailed accounting of the siege, battle, and occupation of Corinth by Union troops. The video is simple but well done and informative. The docents are very knowledgeable, helpful, and will gladly give you all the information and maps you need to make the most of your experience. They can provide you with materials for self-guided walking or driving tours of the city.

Corinth National Cemetery
Horton Street
Open daily: 8 a.m. – 4 p.m.

Here you'll find the gravesites of 1,793 known and 3,895

unknown Civil War soldiers from 15 states. Staring across this wide-open space at the thousands of simple markers is awesome, in the original sense of the word.

**Corinth Civil War Hiking/
Biking Trail**
800-748-9048
www.corinth.net
Open 24 hours a day (restroom facilities open 7 a.m. – 8 p.m.)
Bring your own bike, or rent one through the local bike shop
Free

This 20-mile trail leads you through two historic counties to more Civil War earthworks. It's generally an easy ride, but there are a few challenging hills here and there.

Curlee House
301 Childs St.
662-287-9501
www.curleehouse.org
Summer: Monday – Saturday:
9 a.m.–5 p.m.
Sunday: 1-5 p.m.
Winter: Monday – Saturday:
9 a.m. – 4 p.m.
Sunday: 1 – 4 p.m.
$2.50 for adults, $1.50 for children

CURLEE HOUSE

Built in 1857, the Curlee House served as Civil War headquarters for three Confederate generals and one Union general. It is said that the Battle of Shiloh was planned here. It's a lovely home, typical of the period, and the costumed docent was full of information. (The kids were more interested, however, in climbing on the Civil War cannon in the yard.)

Northeast Mississippi Museum
204 Fourth St. at Washington St., 662-287-3120
Summer: Monday – Saturday: 10 a.m. – 5 p.m.
Sunday: 11 a.m. – 5 p.m.
Winter: Tuesday – Saturday: 10 a.m. – 4:30 p.m.
Sunday: 11 a.m. – 4:30 p.m.
Donations welcome.

You'll find a range of exhibits and artifacts here that further illustrate the impact of the Civil War. There's a photography exhibit as well, plus 20th-century memorabilia. We gathered lots of brochures and a few books here, while the boys were fascinated by the weapons and ammo on display.

This museum is relocating sometime in mid-2006 to the old train depot, which is undergoing a $9 million renovation.

Pick Your Own

There are several places around Corinth where you and the kids can pick'n'purchase your own fresh fruits and berries.

Blueberry Patch
Off Highway 2/County Road 502
662-286-3534
Berries are ripe for picking June – August

Crum's Peach Orchard
Off Highway 2/Kossuth, County Rd. 622
662-462-5125
Peaches, nectarines, and apples: June - October

GRACELAND TOO

Hilltop Peach Farm
Off Hwy 2/Kossuth, County Rd. 620
662-287-9368, 662-665-0817
Peaches, nectarines, and apples: June - October

Hernando
(20 miles from Memphis)

Hernando Courthouse
2535 Highway 51 South
662-429-1460
Monday – Friday: 8 a.m. – 5 p.m.

Built in 1836, this handsome structure is noted for its large wall murals, which depict Hernando de Soto and his discovery of the area in 1541-42. Some of the courtroom scenes from the movie *The People vs. Larry Flynt* were shot here. A nice 10-minute stop.

Holly Springs
(40 miles from Memphis)

Graceland Too
200 E. Gholson Avenue
662-252-2515
www.rockabillyhall.com
/ElvisLives.html
Open 24 hours a day, year-round.
$5 a person

Truly one-of-a-kind. Housed in a smallish antebellum home (nearly 150 years old), this is also the private residence of Elvis' most devoted fan, Paul B. MacLeod. Literally every nook and cranny is filled with Elvis memorabilia. You'll find it fascinating in a surreal sort of way. Your kids might think it is just plain weird. I'll say this, though: I'll never forget it, and I've never spoken to anyone who was disappointed.

Hill Crest Cemetery
Elder Avenue at Market St.
662-252-1515
Open daily: dawn until dusk

Burial site of 13 Confederate generals, plus heroes and heroines of the 1878 yellow fever epidemic, and the first African-American U.S. senator. The engravings on the tombstones tell many stories.

Holly Springs Walking/ Driving Tour
104 East Gholson Avenue
662-252-2515
www.visithollysprings.org
Monday – Friday: 8 a.m. – 5 p.m.
Saturday: 10 a.m. - noon
Call for prices

This is an easy and enjoyable way to get a feel for the town. You'll see seven historic homes, three historic churches, plus other points of interest like the picturesque town square. A number of movies have been shot in Holly Springs.

Holly Springs Historic Path System
154 South Memphis Street
662-252-2943
Map available at the Chamber of Commerce

This walking/driving tour is much more extensive, featuring 84 historic homes (among other things). Many of these homes and other historic buildings are open to the public during the annual Pilgrimage in April (see Annual Events section).

Ida B. Wells Barnett Museum
220 N. Randolph Street
662-252-3232
www.visithollysprings.org
Monday – Friday: 10 a.m. – 5 p.m.
Saturday: noon – 5 p.m.
Closed Sunday
$3 donation for adults,
$2 for students
Groups of 10 or more:
Call for reservations

The historic Spires Bolling home is the birthplace of famed journalist and activist Ida B. Wells. It is also where you'll find collections of artworks by African and African-American artists along with artifacts and historical documents. Ida B. Wells was a fascinating woman whose influence was felt far beyond the city limits of Holly Springs. It's worth learning more about her life as well as viewing the paintings and other artworks here.

Kate Freeman Clark Art Gallery
300 East College Avenue
662-252-4211
By appointment.

Kate Freeman was another fascinating personality from Holly Springs. She was the grandniece of Confederate general Edward Carey Walthall. She studied art in New York and was a prolific and gifted painter. Very few people knew of her talent until after her death, because she never displayed or sold her work. This gallery features 1,050 of her paintings in addition to paintings by William Merrit Chase.

Marshall County Historical Museum
220 East College Avenue
662-252-3669
Monday – Friday: 10 a.m. – 5 p.m.

Definitely one of the better small-town museums. Three stories worth of displays include relics of 11 wars, antique toys, farm tools, county wildlife, Indian artifacts, photography, and more. My favorite displays are of the beautiful antique clothing, some of which date back to the Civil War.

Montrose & Montrose Arboretum
335 East Salem Avenue
662-252-2515
By appointment only
$6 per person

If you like touring historic homes, this one is a beauty. It is a classic, antebellum, brick mansion, which is a prime example of Greek Revival architecture, c. 1858. The Arboretum Society is also located here, featuring 50 different varieties of indigenous trees.

Phillips Grocery
541 East Vandorn Avenue
662-252-4641
Monday – Thursday: 9 a.m. – 5 p.m.
Friday and Saturday: 9 a.m. – 6 p.m.

I love this place! We often make the 30-to-40-minute drive for lunch, which features one of the best hamburgers in the world (or at least, according to *USA Today*, one of the 10 best burgers in America) as well as fried green tomatoes and other treats. Phillips Grocery occupies a 19th-century building adjacent to a train track. Rumor has it that the place used to be a hotel, then a brothel, before becoming a grocery store, then a restaurant. The rustic décor and early 1900s memorabilia add an extra special touch. Be sure to get a Moon Pie and an RC Cola.

Rust College
155 Rust Avenue
662-252-2491
www.rustcollege.edu
By appointment

While it may not be a tourist attraction in the literal sense, it's worth driving by for a look-see (or to apply for admission). Established in 1866 to provide an education to freed slaves, Rust College is a highly respected institution with a rich history and many distinguished graduates. The campus is home to more than 400 pieces of African art, sculptures, and masks, which you are invited to view — just call ahead.

Strawberry Plains Audubon Center
Off Mississippi Highway 331
north of Holly Springs
662-252-1155
www.msaudubon.com/spac.htm
Tuesday – Saturday: 8 a.m. – 4 p.m. (no tours after 3 p.m.)

House tours given on Saturdays at 10 a.m. and 2 p.m.
Nature center and gardens: $3 for adults, $1 for kids 5-11, children under 5 free
House tour: $5 for adults, $3 for kids 5-11, children under 5 free

One of Holly Springs' newest attractions, it's where history and nature come together. This bird and wildlife sanctuary includes two antebellum homes, built in 1852, on nearly 3,000 acres. In addition to hiking and bird watching, guests can tour the Davis home or visit a family-owned, African-American cemetery, which serves as the final resting place for those who actually worked on the plantation.

Walter Place
330 West Chulahoma Avenue
662-252-2515
www.visithollysprings.org
By appointment
$7.50 per person

What a fabulous house! It's huge and ornate. It's filled with breathtaking antiques (with a stunning collection of silver in the dining room). And it has lots of stories to tell. The house served as the temporary home of General and Mrs. Ulysses S. Grant (and at least one of Mrs. Grant's slaves) in 1862. Walter Place has one of the most wonderful porches I have ever seen. It makes you want to don a large straw hat and sip on a mint julep – whether you like mint juleps or not.

Yellow Fever House
104 East Gholson Avenue
662-252-2515
www.visithollysprings.org
Monday – Friday: 8:30 a.m. – 5 p.m.
Saturday: 10 a.m. – noon
Free

Holly Springs' first house built of brick, this home went on to gain greater significance as the residence of W. J. L. Holand, a martyr of the 1878 yellow fever epidemic.

Yellow Fever Martyrs Church Museum
305 East College Avenue
662-252-7552
www.visithollysprings.org
By appointment

This quaint old church has been preserved and converted into a museum to tell the story of the yellow fever epidemic, which ravaged Holly Springs and the entire Mid-South. It's a tragic but mesmerizing time in the region's history.

Natchez Trace Parkway
See the Tupelo listing

New Albany
(80 miles from Memphis)

Union County Heritage Museum
112 Cleveland Street
888-534-8332
Monday – Friday: 10 a.m. – 5 p.m.
Saturday: By appointment

OXFORD

There is a timeline that clearly illustrates the history of Union County to the present day. There are also displays that explain the town's pride in being the birthplace of Nobel Prize winning author William Faulkner, one of America's most famous writers. Additionally, there are exhibits on the Chickasaw Native-American culture, pioneers, and the area's major industry: furniture.

Olive Branch
(Just south of Memphis)

Brussel's Bonsai Nursery
8365 Center Hill Road
901-521-8187
www.brusselsbonsai.com
Monday-Friday: 8 a.m. - 5 p.m.

The largest bonsai "farm" in the U.S. In addition to nurturing and selling these living artworks you'll learn about how they're grown. On Memorial Day weekend, the nursery hosts a "Rendezvous" with bonsai growers from all over the country.

Oxford
(75 miles from Memphis)
www.touroxfordms.com

Center for the Study of Southern Culture
University of Mississippi Campus
662-915-5993
Monday - Friday: 8 a.m. - 5 p.m.

Housed in a fully restored, antebellum observatory, this renowned research center provides an almost mind-boggling amount of information on Southern music, history, folklore, literature, and more. The young child and middle-schooler will not be able to appreciate all that is available here, but the older scholar might.

Historic Town Square
Courthouse Square
800-758-9177
www.touroxfordms.com

The LaFayette County Courthouse & the City Hall are open from 8 a.m. until 5 p.m., Monday to Friday, but the lovely Courthouse Square is yours to stroll anytime. Every block offers historic buildings filled with unique shops, galleries, and restaurants (see separate listings for Southside Gallery and Square Books). As you venture past the square, maybe toward the University of Mississippi (Ole Miss) campus, you'll discover that Oxford is an old town that predates the Civil War and has many lovely homes to show for it. It is also an energetic, stimulating, college town. Oxford is the home of a number of notable writers, including William Faulkner, Willie Morris, and John Grisham.

Ole Miss Blues Archive
University of Mississippi -
Farley Hall
662-232-7753
www.olemiss.edu/depts/general_library
Open Monday - Friday: 9 a.m. - 5 p.m.

For the music lover, specifically the blues lover: the Ole Miss Blues Archive offers an extensive collection of recordings, reference books, and memorabilia, including many personal items of the legendary B.B. King.

Rowan Oak
(Home of William Faulkner)
Old Taylor Rd.
662-234-3284
Tuesday - Saturday: 10 a.m. - 4 p.m.
Sunday: 1-4 p.m.
$5 suggested donation

Visit the famed 1840s home of noted author William Faulkner. He lived here from 1930 until his death in 1962. A lovely, cypress-lined walk leads you up to the old home, which is filled with original furnishings and personal belongings. You can even see Faulkner's outline for his novel A Fable scribbled in his own handwriting on the study wall. The grounds are beautiful, too, and there are outbuildings that are worthy of exploration.
NOTE: William Faulkner is buried at St. Peter's Cemetery, Jefferson at North 16th Street.

Southside Gallery
150 Courthouse Square
662-234-9090
www.southsideoxford.com
Monday - Thursday: 9 a.m. - 9 p.m.
Friday and Saturday: 10 a.m. - 9:30 p.m.

One of Oxford's most popular "hang-outs," the Southside Gallery presents original works from the South and the Caribbean, including folk art and contemporary works, photography, and sculpture. The regularly scheduled openings of each new show always draw big crowds.

Square Books
160 Courthouse Square
662-236-2262
www.squarebooks.com
Monday - Thursday: 9 a.m. - 9 p.m.
Friday and Saturday: 9 a.m. - 10 p.m.
Sunday: 10 a.m. - 6 p.m.

Located in one of the first buildings built in Oxford after the Civil War (c. 1870) — and just up the street from the Southside Gallery and several fantastic restaurants — Square Books is an Oxford landmark. It's privately owned and offers the assistance of a friendly and very knowledgeable staff. Wander upstairs for a muffin or a cup of tea or coffee, then grab a seat and just read and relax. You might want to perch on the upstairs veranda. Square Books invites you to linger — and you never know what famous author might just saunter by.

There are now two other Square Books outlets, also on the Square: Off-Square Books, which carries discounted titles, and the children's bookstore, Square Books Jr.

NATCHEZ TRACE PARKWAY

University Museums
University Avenue and Fifth Street
662-915-7073
www.olemiss.edu/depts/u_museum
Tuesday – Saturday:
10 a.m. – 4:30 p.m.
Sunday: 1 – 4 p.m.
Free, but donations welcome

There's an interesting mix of exhibits here: 18th-and 19th-century scientific apparatuses, Greek and Roman antiquities, Southern folk art, paintings by Theora Hamblett, and revolving exhibits. The Walton Young Historic House is open for tours on Fridays.

Ventress Hall
University of Mississippi Campus
662-915-7236 (media relations)
Monday – Friday: 8 a.m. – 5 p.m.
Free

Tiffany stained-glass windows depict a "mustering of the Greys," students who fought for the Confederacy during the Civil War. Nearby is a small cemetery where Confederate soldiers killed at the Battle of Shiloh are buried.

Tupelo
(104 miles from Memphis)

Elvis Presley Birthplace
306 Elvis Presley Drive
662-841-1245
**May – September: Monday –
Saturday:** 9 a.m. – 5:30 p.m.
**October – April: Monday –
Saturday:** 9 a.m. – 5 p.m.
Open Sundays: 1 – 5 p.m.,
year-round
House: $2.50 for adults, $1.50 for kids 7-12, under 7 free
Museum: $6 for adults, $3 for kids 7-12, under 7 free

Yes, this modest two-room house is the actual birthplace of the "King of Rock'n'Roll." This is where it all began. There is an adjacent park, museum, memorial chapel, and of course, a gift shop.

**Natchez Trace Parkway &
Natchez Trace Visitor Center**
1-800-305-7417
www.scenictrace.com

Beautiful and historic, the famous Natchez Trace connects Natchez, Mississippi, with Nashville. Speed limit: 50 m.p.h. Historic markers along the way explain the history of the Trace from its days as an Indian trade route to its role in the migration of pioneers. Explorer Meriwether Lewis is buried along this trail at milepost #385, and there are numerous other points of interest.

You'll enjoy the scenery, while there are a few places to stop for the kids to get in some tubing, canoeing, and hiking, too.

**Private John Allen
National Fish Hatchery**
111 Elizabeth Street
662-842-1341
Open daily: 7 a.m. – 3:30 p.m.

I know this will hold your kid's attention for a while. Millions of fish are produced here every year, and it's fascinating to see how they are bred and grown. (I like the fact that this place opens at 7 a.m., so you can get a real jump on your day.) There's a quaint Victorian house (the manager's house) and a Grandmother's Garden.

Tupelo Buffalo Park
2272 N. Coley Road
866-27BISON
www.tupelobuffalopark.com
Monday – Saturday: 9 a.m. – 4 p.m.
Sunday: 1 – 4 p.m.

Monday – Thursday:
$8 per adult, $6 per child
Friday – Sunday: $10 per adult, $8 per child
* Or: $25 + tax per family

As if seeing gazillion fish isn't enough, how about a peek at the largest buffalo herd east of the Mississippi River? There's a bus tour that leads you through the

ELVIS PRESLEY BIRTHPLACE

TUPELO BUFFALO PARK

TUPELO AUTOMOBILE MUSEUM

TUPELO NATIONAL BATTLEFIELD

Confederate general Nathan Bed-ford Forrest and Union general William T. Sherman. While you're in the neighborhood, you might want to tour the Brice Cross Roads battlefield as well on Mississippi Highway 370, near Baldwyn.

Tombigbee State Park
264 Cabin Drive
800-467-2757
www.mdwfp.com
Open year-round
$2 per vehicle (50 cents per person over four passengers)
50 cents for walkers and cyclists, $2 for motorcyclists
Cabin rentals range from $45 to $75 a night, depending on availability. Fishing boat rentals are $5 a day, paddleboats cost $3 an hour.

grazing ground, and after the ride, the kids can enjoy a wide assort-ment of animals at the petting zoo.

Tupelo Automobile Museum
1 Otis Boulevard
800-533-0611
Tuesday – Sunday: 10 a.m. – 6 p.m.

More than 150 automobiles are on display, including what is reportedly the world's first auto-mobile: an 1886 motorized car-

riage created by Karl Bentz. Most kids find this pretty intriguing, and the collection is impressive.

Tupelo National Battlefield
2680 Natchez Trace Parkway
800-305-7417
Open daily: dawn until dusk

In July of 1864, the last major battle fought in Mississippi took place here between two of the Civil War's most famous generals:

Outdoor recreation abounds with cabins, developed and primitive camping, canoeing, tubing, fishing, a nature trail, and picnic area.

Annual Events:
Batesville
Fall Festival & Art Mart
(October): 888-872-6652

Byhalia
**White Oak Classic Walking &
Racking Horse Show** (May):
662-838-8127
White Oak Fall Festival
(October): 662-838-2806

Coldwater
Trade Days Flea Market (June,
August, October): 662-562-8715

Corinth
Jacinto Festival (July 4th):
662-286-8662
Slugburger Festival (July):
877-347-0545
www.corinth.ms
**Magnolia Classic Walking Horse
Show** (July):
800-748-9048
Mississippi Tri-State Fair
(September):
662-287-7779
www.crossroadsarena.com
**Hog Wild Corinth Barbecue
Festival** (October):
662-287-7779
www.crossroadsarena.com
Curlee House Heritage Festival
(October):
662-287-9501
www.curleehouse.org

Holly Springs
Holly Springs Pilgrimage (April):
662-252-3260
www.visithollysprings.org/
pilgrimage.html
Kudzu Festival (June):
662-252-2943
**Ida B. Wells Arts & Crafts
Family Festival** (July):
662-252-3232
**National Audubon Society
Annual Hummingbird Migration
Celebration** (September):
662-252-1155
**Annual Open All-Age & Derby
Fitch Farm-Galena Plantation
Field Trial** (December):
662-252-8855
www.fitchfarms.com

New Albany
**Union County Fair & Livestock
Show** (late July-early August):

662-534-1916

Olive Branch
**MayFest Arts & Crafts Fair &
Bluegrass Festival in Old Towne**
(May):
662-893-5276
www.olivebrancholdtowne.com

Oxford
Oxford Conference for the Book
(April):
662-915-5993
www.olemiss.edu/depts/south
**Oxford Double Decker Arts
Festival** (April):
800-758-9177
www.doubledeckerfestival.com
**Annual Faulkner &
Yoknapatawpha Conference**
(July): 662-915-5993
www.outreach.olemiss.edu/
events/faulkner

Senatobia
Mayfair (May):
662-562-8715

Tupelo
Elvis Presley Festival (June):
888-273-7798
Blue Suede Cruise (May):
800-533-0611

The Delta Region
(at least, the northern part of it)

Flat 'n' famous. The Delta has
some of the richest land in the
world — and a hot and humid cli-
mate — which is why so many huge
cotton plantations sprang up
here. Cotton is still "white gold,"
though other crops are bountiful,
too, especially that popular new-
comer, catfish.

With the plantations came slavery, segregation, and the rise of
the Blues, the music for which this
region is famous. The Delta blues
attracts fans from all over the
world in search of juke joints and
festivals. This is where you'll find
some of the best Southern-style
home cooking anywhere: BBQ,
fried catfish, fried chicken, fried

green tomatoes (the operative
word being "fried"), plus greens,
cornbread, biscuits, and of
course, sweet tea.

The Delta is also where you'll
find more of Mississippi's famous
literary and artistic communities,
some of which were nurtured by
strong whiskey and Southern
belles, the Delta's famous debu-
tante balls and sharecropper
cook-outs.

Just a tad beyond my 100-mile
limit, you'll find some very worthwhile places to visit. If you have the
time and inclination, venture farther south to Greenville,
Greenwood, Leland, Cleveland, and
Yazoo City. Even the tiniest communities like Marigold, Sunflower,
and Itta Bena (among others) have
interesting things to offer.

As I said before, Mississippi is
complicated. Let it draw you in.

Clarksdale
(74 miles from Memphis)
www.clarksdale.com

CLARKSDALE TRAIN STATION

Clarksdale Train Station
200 Blues Alley
800-626-3764
Monday - Saturday

A historic passenger depot from
the 1920s is the focal point of this
combination specialty shopping
and dining area attraction. Locals
and visitors alike frequent the
shops here. The Dutch Oven feeds
its loyal following Tuesday —
Saturday starting at 7 a.m. (soups,
sandwiches, and salads, plus fresh-

baked pies and breads, which are to die for! Sorry, no supper). This is just part of a large area that started to develop in recent years, centered around Clarksdale's biggest claim to fame: the blues.

Delta Blues Museum
#1 Blues Alley
800-626-3764
www.deltabluesmuseum.com
Monday – Saturday:
March – October: 9 a.m. – 5 p.m.
November – February:
10 a.m. – 5 p.m.
$6 for adults, $3 for children 6 to 12, free for 6 and under

DELTA BLUES MUSEUM

The Delta Blues Museum features a nice collection of blues artifacts and memorabilia, illustrating the role of the area's cotton culture in the evolution of this uniquely American music. It's a small museum but a very popular one.

Ground Zero Blues Club
Zero Blues Alley
662-621-9009
www.groundzerobluesclub.com
Open for lunch:
Monday – Saturday: 11 a.m. – 2 p.m.
Open for dinner:
Wednesday – Saturday:

5 p.m. – until the crowd goes home
Live music: Every Friday and Saturday night, every other Wednesday night

Just a short walk from Madidi (see separate listing), you'll find Ground Zero, a popular blues club and casual eatery that is also owned by Morgan Freeman and partners. Memorabilia and knick-knacks adorn the walls. It's a great juke joint atmosphere. There are several pool tables and a long bar. The live entertainment, from my experience, is heavy on blues and blues rock. And there's plenty of

HOPSON PLANTATION & SHACK-UP INN

good food on the menu. I really like their burgers. Kid-friendly (at least until around 9 p.m.).

Hopson Plantation & Shack-Up Inn
8141 Old Highway 49
662-624-5756
Commissary, by appointment
Reservations required for Shack-Up Inn

Once the largest cotton farming operation in the Delta, this was also the first farm to produce a cotton crop entirely by machinery (from planting to baling). Nowadays, instead of depending on crops for its

GROUND ZERO BLUES CLUB

success, it has made a name for itself as a unique place for visitors. Guests actually stay in renovated tenant shacks (complete with front porches to perch on). They also enjoy browsing through the antiques and Mississippi Delta artifacts found in the old commissary (on-site). Trust me, this place is one-of-a-kind.

Madidi Restaurant
164 Delta Avenue
662-627-7770
www.madidires.com
Tuesday – Saturday: Bar opens at 5 p.m., dinner starts at 6 p.m.

This upscale restaurant has become an attraction in its own right because the food is delicious. The ambience is sophisticated yet down home, and it's located in an old, historic building. Madidi attracts diners from as far away as Memphis and Oxford because of its famous owner: Oscar-winning actor Morgan Freeman, who lives in a nearby town. His wife, Myrna,

painted many of the original artworks on the walls.

Muddy Waters Cabin Site & Marker
Stovall Road
800-626-3764
Drive by only

For the serious blues enthusiast, a marker locates where legendary bluesman Muddy Waters grew up. The original cabin that once stood here (on the Stovall Plantation) is now on display at the Delta Blues Museum.

St. George's Episcopal Parsonage Church
106 Sharkey Avenue
662-627-7875
Drive by

A little know fact: famous playwright Tennessee Williams spent his childhood in Clarksdale and lived in this parsonage. It now serves as a church office.

W.C. Handy Home Site & Marker
317 Issaquena Avenue
800-626-3764
Drive by only

Before he moved to Memphis and became known worldwide as the "Father of the Blues," W.C. Handy lived on this site from 1903 to 1905.

Tunica
(35 miles from Memphis)

Casinos
Various locations along Highway 61 North, clearly marked

Where they used to grow cotton, they now grow casinos. Nine big-name gaming facilities dot the landscape, making Tunica the third-largest casino center in the U.S. In addition to the various gaming and hotel options, all the casinos offer restaurants, famous entertainers, and all the other amenities one expects of a Vegas-like experience.

Many of the casinos offer day care and night care with special entertainment for the kids. We have taken Will to see special shows like *Cirque de Soleil* and one of the better-known magicians, but we have never dropped him off at one of the children's centers, so I can't give a firsthand recommendation on this service.

Bluesville/Blues & Legends Hall of Fame Museum
1021 Casino Center Drive
800-303-7463
www.horseshoe.com
Open daily: 10 a.m. – 9 p.m.

Located inside the Horseshoe Casino, Bluesville is a 1,200-seat nightclub that features big-name blues, country, and rock performances. There is also a blues museum that includes the Bluesville Dry Goods Gallery and Gift Shop.

Tunica Museum
4063 Highway 61 North
662-363-6631
www.tunicamuseum.com
**Tuesday, Wednesday, Friday,
Saturday:** 10 a.m. – 5 p.m.
Thursday: 10 a.m. – 9 p.m.
Sunday: 1–5 p.m.
Free

Tunica was a poor agricultural community before becoming one of the nation's leading casino centers. This small museum presents the history of Tunica County from its early beginnings, when the land was covered in hardwood forests, through its heyday as a cotton center, to the present.

Tunica Queen Riverboat
RiverPark Drive, just off Fitzgeralds Boulevard before Fitzgeralds Casino
662-363-7622, 866-805-3535
www.tunicaqueen.com
Call for seasonal schedules
Cruise: Adults - $19.50,
Kids - $14.50
River Lore Cruise: Adults - $12,
Kids - $7
**Dinner & Entertainment Cruise:
Sunday – Thursday:** $34.50
Friday & Saturday: $37.50
Special dockside events and holiday cruises

Tunica's newest attraction, along with the RiverPark (see below), this 300-passenger pad-dle wheeler features three decks. The mezzanine or lower level offers dining and dancing. The top level offers an open-air view of the stars. Food, music, and the Mississippi River combine for a memorable experience, and the kids will enjoy an excursion that's casual and comfortable.

Tunica RiverPark Museum
RiverPark Drive, just off Fitzgeralds Boulevard, just before Fitzgeralds Casino
662-357-0050
Open 7 days a week:
9 a.m. – 6 p.m.
Cost: $5 for adults, $4 for children

This new attraction offers a diversion from the nearby gaming with a focus on the geological and anthropological history of the area. A $24 million facility, the museum sits on the edge of the Mississippi River. Exhibits tell the story of the region's flora and fauna, its early civilizations and explorations, pioneers, the riverboat, and cotton cultures.

Blue & White Restaurant - $
1355 U.S. 61 North
662-363-1371

Homemade donuts and pies, country vegetables, hamburger steak smothered in onions, turkey and dressing, and turnip greens. Since 1937, when this place was a gas station and eatery (the Greyhound Bus still stops here), the Blue & White Restaurant has been a landmark. All the cooking is done from scratch. Visitors can enjoy a cup of coffee and stay as long as they like. It's old-fashioned, Southern-style dining, and it's worth a stop and a bite — especially for the daily noon buffet.

Annual Events

Clarksdale
Delta Jubilee & Barbecue-Cooking Contest (June)
800-626-3764
www.clarksdale.com
Sunflower River Blues & Gospel Festival (August)
662-627-2209
Tennessee Williams Festival (October)
800-626-3764
www.clarksdale.com

Tunica
The Maker's Market Gift Show of the Delta (March)
662-363-3336
Rivergate Festival & BBQ Cooking Contest (April)
662-363-2865

* There are lots of horse shows, rodeos, and other equestrian events in Tunica. For information on these, contact the Tunica Convention & Visitors Bureau at 888-488-6422, www.tunicamiss.org.

Tennessee
General Vacation Information:
www.TNvacation.com
800-GO2-TENN

African-American Guide to Cultural and Historic Sites
888-243-9769
Tennessee State Parks
888-TNPARKS
www.tnstateparks.com
* There are 12 state parks in West Tennessee
Civil War Trails
615-532-1550
Tennessee Wildlife Resources Agency
800-372-3928

FYI: Tennessee is divided into three primary regions:

West Tennessee, Middle Tennessee, and East Tennessee
I've focused exclusively on major highlights within the West Tennessee Plains.

West Tennessee

West Tennessee is very different from the rest of the state. Its flatlands are a sharp contrast to the hills and mountains found to the east. West Tennessee is known for blues and rock'n'roll, not bluegrass or country music. I think it's fair to say that West Tennesseans have more in common with nearby Mississippians than with their fellow statesmen. Their region is a product of the cotton culture, of plantations and slavery, of yellow fever epidemics, and Mississippi River commerce. While West Tennessee fell to Federal troops in the early years of the Civil War, it remained staunchly Confederate while there were some parts of East Tennessee that held

> **∽ LITTLE KNOWN FACT:** Tennessee is surprisingly long, east to west. In fact, Bristol, Tennessee, is closer to Canada than it is to Memphis!

strong, pro-Union sentiments. So much for the differences…

West Tennessee is for music lovers. Millions of people travel from all over the world to see attractions related to musicians like Elvis Presley, W.C. Handy, B.B. King, "Sleepy" John Estes, and Carl Perkins, pioneers in blues, rock'n'roll, soul, gospel, and rhythm'n'blues. But once visitors arrive, they discover there's a whole lot more.

West Tennessee is also the home of antebellum grandeur and the struggle for civil rights, Civil War battlefields and professional sports, fine art museums and country crafts. While West Tennessee doesn't offer the range of outdoor recreation found in the hills and mountains elsewhere in the state, there are plenty of nature trails, lakes, and rivers full of recreational activities. (Some people say you haven't lived until you've kayaked on the Mississippi River at sunset.)

My ancestors came to West Tennessee in the 1820s. We stayed because we like it here. I think you will, too.

I would be remiss if I didn't mention that there are some really cool places to visit that are a bit beyond my "100-miles from Memphis" limit. Reelfoot Lake (straight up Highway 51 North) is very interesting — and it's where you'll find the annual Eagle Tours each January (the first place in the country to offer such a thing). Paris, Tennessee, 800-345-1103, offers its very own Eiffel Tower — "only one Paris has a taller Eiffel Tower." Continue traveling northeast, past Paris, to Camden for the Tennessee River Freshwater Pearl Farm (tours of 15 or more people, or by special arrangement, available through the Birdsong Resort Marina, 800-225-7469). Other notable offerings include the Pioneer Homestead in Dyer, Milan's West Tennessee Agricultural Museum, and the Davy Crockett Cabin & Museum in Rutherford. And this is just the tip of the iceberg...

Adamsville
(100 miles from Memphis)

Buford Pusser Home & Museum
342 Pusser Street
731-632-4080
Monday – Saturday: 9 a.m. – 5 p.m.
Sunday (May 1 – October 31): noon – 6 p.m
(November 1 – April 30): 1 – 5 p.m.
$5 for adults, $2 for students
Tour length: 1 hour

Made famous in the *Walking Tall* movie series, Sheriff Buford Pusser was a shy but tough lawman — the stuff legends are made of. This home is where he lived until his death in 1974. The home's original furnishings and memora-

BROWNSVILLE TIDBIT:
Also known as the Taylors of Tabernacle, the annual Taylor Kinfolk Camp Meeting, held just outside of town, is one of the oldest and largest, ongoing family reunions in the country. A tradition that began in 1826, the weeklong reunion attracts hundreds of cousins from all over the world to visit the family's ancestral land, which includes cabins, a church, and a private cemetery.

bilia attest to Pusser's unusual career in law enforcement. During his tenure, he was shot eight times, knifed seven times, fought six men at the same time (and won), destroyed 87 whiskey stills, and performed other acts of daring. He died in a car crash (many suspect foul play) following a Memphis press conference where he announced he would play himself in a fourth Buford Pusser movie. (See Selmer listing.)

* For an added treat, grab a bite to eat in town at the Pusser Restaurant, owned and operated by Dwana Pusser Garrison.

Brownsville
(58 miles from Memphis)

Billy Tripp Minefield
One Mindfield Alley
731-772-2193
www.brownsville-haywoodtn.com
Drive by only

The Minefield can be considered a source of controversy or pride, depending on your point of view. Local artist and welder Billy Tripp began assembly of this giant metal structure/sculpture a number of years ago, and it continues to be a work in progress. He just keeps adding to it; I think it's about 75 feet tall for now. It's too abstract to describe; you just need to see it for yourself. I find it fascinating — a lot more interesting than the world's largest ball of twine, which might be the kind of thing you'd compare it to.

Haywood County Museum and High School Sports Museum
College Hill Center
127 N. Grand Avenue
731-772-4883 or 772-2193
www.brownsville-haywoodtn.com
Open Monday, Wednesday – Friday: 10 a.m. – 4 p.m.
Sunday: 2 – 4 p.m.
Free

Dividing its history into 25-year segments, this museum traces the past of Haywood County from its earliest Native-American residents to the present. There are military uniforms, lots of historical photos, and antique tools. The Sports Museum salutes the county's high school sports teams and individual players who went on to statewide or national prominence. And a wonderful surprise: the Abraham Lincoln Collection, an impressive array of artifacts on the American president, which was amassed by the late Morton Felsenthal and his father.

Delta Heritage Center
111 N. Washington
(just north of I-40, exit 56)
731-779-9000
www.brownsville-haywoodtn.com
Open daily from 9 a.m.-7 p.m.
Free

A highlight of this regional information center is the humble home of famed blues musician Sleepy John Estes. Just a few feet away, the main building includes various galleries of historical memorabilia that present the history of the area's music, cotton industry, and Hatchie River wildlife. West Tennessee tourist information is also available on-site. It's a nice diversion (and I've bought some nice pottery in the gift shop).

Covington
(39 miles from Memphis)

The Ruffin Theater & South Main Historic District
Theater: East Pleasant
476-9727
Chamber of Commerce
476-9727
www.covingtontn.com

The Ruffin Theater is a lovely Art Deco facility built in 1937. Currently it's used as a venue for the performing arts. While you're in town, tour the rest of Covington, too. There are 52 homes and other structures of picturesque appeal and historic significance, many of which are listed on the Historic Register.

Tipton County Museum, Veterans Memorial & Nature Center
751 Bert Johnson Avenue
476-0242
tcmuseum@yahoo.com
Open Tuesday-Friday: 9 a.m.-5 p.m.
Saturday: 10 a.m. – 4 p.m.
Closed Sunday and Monday
Free

Offering a unique combination of themed attractions, this muse-

AMES PLANTATION

um, memorial, and nature center includes the Covington Wildlife Sanctuary and Nature Trail, a new Nature Center, and a display of artifacts honoring the area's veterans. The Veterans Museum makes for an interesting excursion.

Fort Pillow State Historic Park
(Roughly 45 miles from Memphis)
828 Park Road (off U.S. Highway 51 and west of State Hwy. 87)
731-738-5581
Open daily: 8 a.m. - 4 p.m.
Free

Fort Pillow is a 1,646-acre park on the Chickasaw Bluffs that overlooks the Mississippi River. You can still see the earthwork remains of a major fortification, which was built here in 1861 by the Confederate Army.

(Fort Pillow is in Lauderdale County, where you will also find worthy attractions in the towns of Henning and Halls. See separate listings.)

AMES PLANTATION

∽ MORE TRIVIA:
Tennessee shares borders with more states than any other, totaling seven in all – Arkansas, Mississippi, Missouri, Kentucky, Virginia, Georgia, and Alabama.

Grand Junction
(Roughly 60 miles from Memphis)

Ames Plantation
4275 Buford Ellington Rd.
878-1067
www.amesplantation.org
Drive by only

NATIONAL BIRD DOG MUSEUM,
FIELD TRIAL HALL OF FAME
& WILDLIFE HERITAGE CENTER

Headquarters for the National Championship for field trialing bird dogs (see below), this gorgeous antebellum home conjures up images of the Old South.

National Bird Dog Museum, Field Trial Hall of Fame & Wildlife Heritage Center
505 West Highway 57
764-2058 or 878-1168
Open Tuesday – Friday:
10 a.m. – 2 p.m.
Saturday: 10 a.m. – 4 p.m.
Sunday: 1 – 4 p.m.
Free

For those who don't know, a field trial is a winter sporting competition in which bird dogs are expected to find and point out covies of quail without scaring them off. The hunters and judges follow the dogs on horseback.

Grand Junction is the home of the National Field Trials, which attract hundreds of hunters, dogs, and spectators each year. The dogs and their owners are all duly honored at the Field Trial Hall of Fame, a facility that salutes more than 40 breeds of bird dogs with exhibits of bird dog art, wildlife murals, and a collection of game birds and other examples of area wildlife.

Tennessee Pewter Company
133 Madison Avenue
800-764-2064
www.tnpewter.com
Monday – Thursday:
10 a.m. – 3 p.m.
Tuesday and Wednesday are best, because the full staff is on-site.

Since 1972, Tennessee artisans have handcrafted more than 500 spun pewter products like goblets, bowls, candlesticks, and other tableware here. Cast pewter items include jewelry, letter openers, and collectibles. It's interesting to see how they work, and most of their goods are for sale.

Halls
(60 miles from Memphis)

Veteran's Museum and Air Show
Co-op Drive (off Highway 51)
731-836-7448
Saturday and Sunday: 2 – 5 p.m. or by appointment (all folks welcome, will gladly open up for you!)
Free
Tour length: 1-2 hours

Located at Arnold Field, former site of a WWII B-17 training base, this museum honors all veterans from all wars but is noted for its WWI and WWII exhibits. Smaller displays honor Korea, Vietnam, and Desert Storm. The big event of the year is held the last weekend in August when the air show comes to town. It features vintage planes, displays, and acrobatic flying.

Henning

(Roughly 45 miles from Memphis)

Alex Haley House Museum
200 S. Church Street
731-738-2240
Tuesday – Saturday
10 a.m. – 5 p.m.
Sunday, 1 –5 p.m.
Adults: $2.50; children under 12: $1

Fred Montgomery, former mayor of Henning and Alex Haley's cousin, offers personal and deeply moving tours of the comfortable, boyhood home of the Pulitzer Prize-winning author. Alex Haley's family history, traced from Africa through the days of slavery on to the present day, became the basis for the best-selling book, *Roots* (later made into the hit TV miniseries). The house was built by Haley's grandfather around 1918 and contains family artifacts, memorabilia, and audio-tapes. The front lawn is Haley's final resting place.

Bethlehem Cemetery
Hwy. 51 North and Hwy. 87 East
731-738-2240
Open daily
dawn until dusk

The Haley family burial plot is located here and includes the final gravesite of Alex Haley's famous ancestor, Chicken George.

Humboldt
(Roughly 80 miles from Memphis)

West Tennessee Regional Art Center
1200 Main Street
731-784-1787
www.wtrac.tn.org
Monday, Wednesday, Friday:
9 a.m. – 4 p.m.
$2 per person

This is a real find. One doesn't expect to meander into a small town and discover this kind of quality art. The center, located in the old City Hall (built in 1912), houses the large and sublime Caldwell collection of 18th-, 19-, and 20th-century oil paintings, sculptures, watercolors, lithographs, and silk screens. Some of the noted artists represented here include Red Grooms, Carroll Cloar, Larry Rivers, and Gilbert Gaul to name a few. There are permanent exhibits as well as rotating and traveling exhibitions. Also housed here is the West Tennessee Strawberry Festival Historical Museum.

ALEX HALEY HOUSE MUSEUM

Summer: Open daily 8 a.m. – 9 p.m.
Winter: Open daily 9 a.m. – 5 p.m.
Closed Easter, Thanksgiving, and
Christmas

Historic 1890s home of America's most legendary railroad man, Casey Jones. Featured are railroad artifacts, an original steam locomotive engine, two 25-foot model railroad exhibits in 1890s railcars, and the Casey Jones Train Store. There is also a miniature train that gives folks rides around Case Jones Village.

Cypress Grove Nature Park
U.S. Highway 70 West
731-425-8364
www.cityofjackson.net
Open 7 days a week
dawn until dusk
Free

A short drive from downtown Jackson, Cypress Grove is a 165-acre preserve of the area's river bottom habitat. An elevated boardwalk extending 7,000 feet takes you through a natural hardwood wetland with more than 175 species of birds. The park is also home to the Aerie Trail Raptor Center, a haven for injured birds of prey (bald eagles, golden eagles, barred owls, great horned owls, red-tailed hawks, black vultures, and turkey vultures). This is a great way to spend an afternoon.

CASEY JONES HOME & RAILROAD MUSEUM

Jackson
(85 miles from Memphis)

**Brooks Shaw & Son
Old Country Store**
Casey Jones Village, I-40 at
Hwy. 45 Bypass, Exit 80A
731-668-1223
www.caseyjonesvillage.com
Summer: Open daily 6 a.m.- 10 p.m.
Winter: Open daily 6 a.m. – 9 p.m.
Closed Easter, Thanksgiving, and
Christmas

Re-creation of a turn-of-the-century country store that displays more than 15,000 antiques and includes a Southern country-themed restaurant with three buffets served daily. There is also an 1890s ice cream parlor and a 6,000 square-foot gift, confectionery, and collectibles shop. Yummy. Kids will love shopping in the country store — plenty of souvenirs. See below for information on the Casey Jones Museum.

**Casey Jones Home &
Railroad Museum**
Casey Jones Village, I-40 at
Hwy. 45 Bypass, Exit 80A
731-668-1222
www.caseyjones.com

LaGrange
(45 miles from Memphis)

LaGrange Historic District
14600 LaGrange Road (City Hall)
878-1246
www.lagrangetn.com
Mostly a driving tour

This quaint antebellum town, often referred to as La Belle Village, offers a walking and driving tour that is steeped in Civil War history and lovely Old South aesthetics. In fact, the entire town has been designated as a historic district and is on the National Register. The main road through town (which starts out as Poplar Avenue in Memphis) is lined with beautiful private homes (not open to the public). Brochures for the self-guided walking tour are available — and it's right on your way to Grand Junction. Nearly 30 landmarks are on view. I never tire of visiting here. Just a few highlights are listed below.

Cogbill's General Store & Museum
14840 LaGrange Road
(corner of Highway 57)
878-1235
Wednesday – Saturday:
10 a.m. – 5 p.m.

The original structure was destroyed by a tornado in 1900, rebuilt in 1901, then destroyed by fire in 1998. Not easily deterred, Cogbill's was rebuilt again in 2000 and continues to thrive. Now this wonderful country store specializes in the wares of 104 artists and antique dealers, mostly locals. Tourists can get local information and history while sippin' on some cold sarsaparillas and sampling the hoop cheese.

Woodlawn
Highway 57 at the far eastern edge of town
Drive by only

There are many lovely antebellum homes in LaGrange, but this is the grandest. Built in 1828 and earning a historic marker, it gives Tara a good run for its money.

Mason
(35 miles from Memphis)

Bozo's BBQ
342 Highway 70
(Summer Avenue out of Memphis)
294-3400
Tuesday – Saturday:
10:30 a.m. – 9 p.m.

Like Gus's World Famous Fried Chicken (see below), Bozo's is in a

league of its own. To the uninformed, it may appear to be a simple roadside BBQ joint, but to those who know, its barbecue is some of the best. Fans from four counties insist it's worth the trip (and about half of them come from Memphis).

Gus's World Famous Fried Chicken
505 Highway 70 West, Mason, TN
294-2028
Open year-round except
Thanksgiving Day &
Christmas Day

More than a restaurant, it's an attraction. There is a Gus's in downtown Memphis now as well as one in Jackson, Tennessee, but this is the original. It offers chicken fried in a famous, spicy batter with all the trimmings (beans, slaw, and great pies). Many Memphians will make the drive for lunch or dinner, just for fun.

> **∽ MILAN TIDBIT:**
> While in Milan, grab a lunch at the Cotton Patch Restaurant. It's a lovely place with friendly service and terrific Southern cooking. Great for all ages.

PICKWICK LANDING STATE PARK

Milan
(95 miles from Memphis)

West Tennessee Agricultural Museum
University of Tennessee
Experiment Station
Highway 70A-79 North
731-686-8067
Monday – Friday: 8 a.m. – 4 p.m.
Saturday: Noon – 4 p.m.
Free
Tour length: 1-2 hours

This is another surprise, and another reason why it's a treat to travel off the beaten path. This museum displays more than 2,600 agrarian artifacts. There are a number of dioramas depicting the waterways and early pioneers, the evolution of the subsistence farmer to that of large commercial farms, early dwellings of farmers, the early schoolhouse, and a blacksmith shop — plus lots and lots of farm equipment from two centuries. The log cabin birthplace of Governor Gordon Brown is on-site, too.

Pickwick Landing State Park
(Roughly 117 miles from Memphis)

Pickwick Dam, TN
Pickwick Resort Inn:
866-646-0388
www.state.tn.us/environment/parks
Highway 57 at Highway 128
Open 7 days a week

On a recent fall break, when the kids were out of school, a friend and I took four boys, ages 8-12, for a two-night stay. We rented a two-bedroom suite at the Pickwick Resort Inn, which included a living room, dining area, and small kitchen. It was perfect. The weather was a bit chilly, but there was an indoor, heated pool plus an arcade. In fair weather, one can play tennis or rent a boat at the nearby marina. In our case, we skipped rocks on the lake, hiked, and played hide'n'seek in the nearby cemetery.

We also took a day trip that included nearby Corinth (20 minutes away) and Shiloh Military Park (10 minutes away). We had dinner one night at the landmark Boatel, a barge on the shore of the Tennessee River that has been converted into a motel and restaurant known for its fried catfish. The kids were fascinated by the dam, which is beautiful at night, covered in lights. This was a really easy and affordable getaway.

Pinson

(Roughly 90 miles from Memphis)

Pinson Mounds State Archaeological Park

460 Ozier Rd. in Pinson
(just south of Jackson)
731-988-5614
www.state.tn.us/environment/parks
Open Monday – Saturday:
8 a.m.- 4:30 p.m.
Sunday: 1-5 p.m.
Free.

This 1,086-acre, prehistoric, Indian ceremonial center contains the second-highest mound in the U.S. Archaeological research is conducted on-site and at the museum. Hiking trails, bicycling, picnic shelters, and a playground are all available year-round.

Savannah

(113 miles from Memphis)

Savannah Historic District & Historic Trail

507 Main Street
1-800-552-FUNN
www.tourhardincounty.org/trail.htm

Savannah is a beautiful town, as picturesque as they come. This two-mile stretch features 16 homes dating from 1830 to 1930. In addition to the views of the Tennessee River, there are interpretive exhibits along the way. Of particular interest are Cherry Mansion, General U.S. Grant's headquarters prior to the Battle of Shiloh, and the interpretation of the "Trail of Tears"

COON CREEK SCIENCE CENTER

Cherokee Indian removal of 1838. The White Elephant bed & breakfast (also known as the Welsh-Nesbitt house) is open to tour by appointment. Brochures are available at the Tennessee River Museum (see below). There used to be a ferry that ran from Savannah, across the Tennessee River, to the historic town of Saltillo (925-2364). It was once operated by Alex Haley, Sr. and his wife, Queen. Sadly, this attraction closed in the fall of 2003, but Saltillo is still worth a visit.

Tennessee River Museum

507 Main Street
1-800-552-FUNN
www.tourhardincounty.org/trm.htm
Open Monday – Saturday:
9 a.m.–5 p.m.
Sunday: 1 – 5 p.m.
Adults: $2.50,
children & students free

The Tennessee River Museum is well-organized and well-presented, showcasing the land, the people, and the heritage of the Tennessee River and Tennessee Valley. The many exhibits cover paleontology, archaeology, steamboats, and the Civil War. It's a worthwhile experience, but a word to the wise: after Corinth and Shiloh, our kids were "OD-ing" on Civil War history. I suggest you make Savannah and Saltillo a day trip of their own.

Selmer

(Roughly 90 miles from Memphis)

Buford Pusser Sheriff's Office

Court Avenue
(Courthouse basement)
731-645-6360
Monday & Tuesday, Thursday – Sunday: 8:30 a.m. – 4:30 p.m.
Closed Wednesdays
Free

Some parents and grandparents will remember the *Walking Tall* movies of the 1970s. They were based on the experiences of the legendary Sheriff Buford Pusser. You can visit the basement of the courthouse and see his office, which includes memorabilia from his storied career. (See Adamsville listing.)

Coon Creek Science Center

Operated by the Memphis Pink Palace Museum
Call for directions:
320-6320, 731-645-6360
Open to the public on special occasions (call for dates) and by appointment for groups of 20 or more.

This is one of my favorite places. It is a fossil site with thousands of fossils of more than 600 species of marine life dating back more than 70 million years.

SHILOH NATIONAL MILITARY PARK

emphasis on early education and the Civil War. Upon entering, you see the theater's original ticket window and flyers from movies of the 1930s. The rest of the museum includes the School Room, War Room, Healing Arts Room, and the Business and Agriculture Room.

Shiloh National Military Park
(Roughly 110 miles from Memphis)
Tennessee Highway 22
(southeast of Selmer, Tennessee, and 22 miles northeast of Corinth, Mississippi)
731-689-5696
www.nps.gov/shil/
Open daily: 8 a.m. – 5 p.m.
Closed Christmas Day
$3 per individual, $5 per family, children 16 and under are free
Tour length: Minimum of one hour for the 9.5-mile drive tour (I'd allow closer to three hours to see it properly)
Picnic area

The Civil War's first major killing field, Shiloh was the second-bloodiest battle of the entire war and a turning point for the South. Nearly 24,000 casualties were suffered in two days of battle on the banks of the Tennessee River (April 6-7, 1862). Arguably the best preserved of the major battlefields. It covers 4,000 acres and offers well-organized guides for driving, hiking, or biking. It's beautiful and deeply moving, especially with landmarks like the Sunken Road and Bloody Pond. Annual living history and reenactment events first weekend in April.

Millions of years ago, much of Tennessee was an ocean bed. Coon Creek is still the site of ongoing archaeological digs, and through an agreement with the Pink Palace Museum in Memphis, families can spend the day collecting fossils. On-site docents show budding scientists how to properly wash and preserve them, too. It's really a memorable experience.

McNairy County Historical Museum
114 N. 3rd Street
731-645-5495
Saturday: 10 a.m. – 4 p.m.
Sunday: 1 – 4 p.m.
Other days by appointment

Located in the historic Ritz Theater building, this museum presents the county's history with

Shiloh Civil War Relics & Museum
Adjacent to Shiloh Military Park
689-4114
www.shilohrelics.com
Monday-Saturday:
9:30 a.m. – 5 p.m.
Sunday: 1 – 5 p.m.
Closed Tuesday

You'll find Hardin County's largest collection of authentic

TRENTON TEAPOT MUSEUM

TIDBIT:
The Kelly Miller Circus is an old-time family circus that tours the small towns of the South every spring. You can bring the kids in the morning and watch the elephant raise the old-fashioned Big Top tent and return later for a very entertaining circus show. It's nothing fancy, but it's very "real." To learn if they are performing around the Mid-South while you're visiting, call 580-326-7511.

Civil War era artifacts at this site, a landmark in its own right. My grandfather took me here when I was young. Children love to browse, and my young boys always leave with a toy sword. Souvenirs just go with the territory.

Trenton
(Roughly 85 miles from Memphis)

Trenton Teapot Museum
309 S. College, City Hall
731-855-2013
www.teapotcollection.com
Monday – Friday: 8 a.m. – 5 p.m.
Free

The world's largest collection of teapots, including 525 rare porcelain Veilleuse-Theieres (nightlight teapots) collected from Asia, Africa, and Europe. Another rare find in an unexpected place.

Annual Events

Adamsville
Buford Pusser Festival (May):
731-632-1401
Brownsville
Brownsville Blues Festival
(September): 731-772-1831,
www.brownsville-haywoodtn.com

Covington
Ruffin Theater Heritage Festival
(September): 476-3439

Dresden
Tennessee Iris Festival
(Last Saturday in April –
1st Saturday in May):
731-364-3787

Grand Junction
National Field Trials
Championship (February):
878-1067

Halls
Wings Over Halls Veteran's
Museum Air Show (August):
731-635-9541

Humboldt
West Tennessee Strawberry
Festival (May):
731-784-1842
www.humboldttnchamber.org
/strawberry.html

Jackson
Casey Jones Old Time Music
Fest (September):
800-748-9588
Casey Jones Train Fest (May):
731-427-1565

Rockabilly Festival (August):
731-423-5440
www.rockabillyhall.org
Shannon Street Blues &
Heritage Festival (June):
731-427-7573
www.downtownjackson.com
Skyfest Tennessee (October):
731-660-1088
www.skyfest.us

Pinson
Pinson Mounds Festival
(September):
731-988-5614

Ripley
Lauderdale County Tomato
Festival (July):
731-635-9541

Savannah
Annual Living History
Demonstration (April):
800-552-3866

Selmer
Jammin' Jamboree (August):
731-645-3428
Broomcorn Festival
(September):
731-645-4823

Shiloh
Annual Living History and
Reenactment (April):
731-689-5696, 800-552-3866
www.tourhardincounty.org

Trenton
Trenton Teapot Festival
(late April-early May)
731-855-2013

CHAPTER 8

Annual Events

Birthday party possibilities, helpful websites, and other useful information

ELVIS TRIBUTE WEEK

Memphis Annual Events

THE FOLLOWING is a partial list-ing of the more than 200 festi-vals and special events held in Memphis each year. Shelby County events are listed, per town, in Chapter Six, and regional events are listed, per community, in Chapter Seven.

January
Elvis Birthday Week
332-3322
www.elvis.com

Blues First Weekend
527-2583
www.blues.org
Dr. Martin Luther King Jr. National Holiday
521-9699

February
Beale Street Zydeco Festival
529-0999
Kroger St. Jude & Cellular South Cup Indoor Tennis Championships
685-ACES
www.krogerstjude.com
Black History Month
543-5333

March
Southern Women's Show
800-849-0248
www.southernshows.com
Memphis International Film Festival
273-0014
www.memphisfilmforum.org

April
Africa in April
947-2133
aiafest@bellsouth.net
Kids Count Family Expo
543-2333

MEMPHIS IN MAY

NASCAR Craftsman Truck Series
866-40-SPEED
www.memphismotorsportspark.com

Germantown Charity Horse Show
754-0009
www.gchs.org

Juneteenth Freedom Festival
385-4943
www.juneteenth.com/4tenn_us.htm

Arts in the Park
212-0239
www.experienceartinmemphis.org

MEMPHIS ITALIAN FESTIVAL

July
Beale Street 4th of July
529-0999

WEVL FM90 Blues
on the Bluff – Part I
528-0560
www.wevl.org

Live at the Garden Concert
& July 4th Celebration
685-1566

Fiesta at the Zoo
276-WILD

August
Choctaw Heritage Festival
785-3160
www.chucalissa.org

Elvis Tribute Week
332-3322
www.elvis.com

WEVL FM90 Blues
on the Bluff – Part II
528-0560
www.wevl.org

Memphis Music & Heritage Festival
525-3655
www.southernfolklore.com

WLOK Stone Soul Picnic
527-9565

Memphis Botanic Garden
Eggstravaganza Egg Hunt
685-1566

May
Memphis in May
525-4611
www.memphisinmay.org
1st weekend: Beale St. Music Festival
2nd weekend: DestiNations International Family Festival
3rd weekend: World Championship BBQ Cooking Contest
4th weekend: Great Southern Food Festival & Sunset Symphony

TSSAA Spring Fling
543-5319

W.C. Handy Blues Awards
547-2583
www.handyawards.com

Cotton Maker's Jubilee
774-1118

FedEx St. Jude Golf Classic
748-0534
www.hushyall.com

June
Ducks Unlimited Great
Outdoors Festival
758-3858

Memphis Italian Festival
767-6949
www.memphisitalianfestival.com

Juneteenth Celebration
458-3950

September

Cooper-Young Festival
276-7222
www.cooperyoung.com
Germantown Festival
757-9212
Central Gardens Home Tour
722-4170
www.centralgardens.com
Southern Heritage Classic
398-6655
www.southernheritageclassic.com
Mid-South Fair
274-1776, 274-8800
www.midsouthfair.com
Taste of Midtown
273-0014
www.overtonsquare.com
International Goat Days
872-4559
www.internationalgoatdays.com
Agricenter's Mid-South Maze
757-7777
www.agricenter.org

October

The Mulberry Fine Arts Festival
853-0442
www.collierville.com
Bartlett Celebration
385-5589
International Freedom Awards
521-9699
www.civilrightsmuseum.org

Pink Palace Crafts Fair
320-6320
www.memphismuseums.org
**NASCAR Busch Series & the NHRA
O'Reilly Mid-South Nationals**
866-40-SPEED
www.memphismotorsportspark.com
Repair Days Weekend and Auction
774-6380
www.metalmuseum.org
**Subsidium Carrousel of
Shoppes** 683-6557
www.subsidium.org
Native American Days
785-3160
www.chucalissa.org
**Botanic Garden
Halloween Harvest Festival**
685-1566
Memphis Zoo Boo
276-WILD

PINK PALACE CRAFTS FAIR

November

W.C. Handy Birthday Celebration
527-3427
W.C. Handy Heritage Awards
527-3427
Enchanted Forest
320-6320

December

AXA Liberty Bowl
795-7700
www.libertybowl.org
Christmas at Graceland
332-3322
www.elvis.com
**Beale Street New Year's
Eve Celebration**
526-0110
Collierville Christmas Parade
853-3223
Christmas in Collierville
853-1666
Germantown Holiday Parade
755-1200
Ballet Memphis' *The Nutcracker*
763-0139
A Christmas Carol
at Theatre Memphis
682-8323
Kwanzaa Celebration
521-9699
Memphis Christmas Parade
575-0540
www.downtownmemphis.com

THE MID-SOUTH FAIR

Summer Concert Series

Family-friendly outdoor concerts abound all summer long. Most of them invite you to bring your own blanket, lawn chair, and picnic basket while others offer a delicious array of dining choices on-site. Star performers range from acoustic to rock to country to — you name it. Some of the larger music series are offered at the following venues:

Dixon Gallery & Gardens
761-5250
www.dixon.org
Live at the Garden
685-1566 x107
Memphis Botanic Garden
685-1566
www.memphisbotanicgarden.com
Mud Island River Park
576-7241
www.mudisland.com

Birthday Party Possibilities

FYI: Virtually all the city's museums and major event venues will gladly work with you to organize a birthday party.

Downtown

AutoZone Park
8 South Third Street
721-6050
What better way to celebrate than with America's favorite pastime! Plus there's the carnival and arcade area. Special group rates and packages available. Fun for any age.

The Fire Museum
118 Adams Avenue
320-5650
Offers a birthday party room. Especially well-suited for younger children (under age 10). Bring your own cake and other refreshments (they can supply the ice).

Jillian's
150 Peabody Place
543-8800
The Hi-Life Bowling Lanes and the Amazing Games Arcade (with snack bar) are very popular sites for parties. Packages available including cake.

Maggie Moo's Ice Cream and Treatery
150 Peabody Place
205-1011
Homemade ice cream, candies, and Moolah Gift Certificates.

Memphis Queen Line
45 Riverside Drive
527-BOAT
Food on-board and sometimes Captain Dale or her crew will let the special guest up into the Pilot House.

Mallory-Neely House or Woodruff-Fontaine House in Victorian Village
652 Adams Avenue
523-1484 and
680 Adams Avenue
526-1469
Great options for little girls who might enjoy an old-fashioned tea party. Catering available.

Mud Island River Park
125 North Front Street
576-7241
Can provide indoor or outdoor facilities. Full-service catering available.

FIRE MUSEUM

Muvico Movie Theatre
150 Peabody Place
248-0100
Private rooms available. $18 per child, weekends only.

Putting Edge
150 Peabody Place
523-0204
www.puttingedge.com
Glow-in-the-dark miniature golf. Party room available. Birthday packages include everything but the cake.

CHILDREN'S MUSEUM OF MEMPHIS

Midtown

Children's Museum of Memphis
2525 Central Avenue
458-4033
Party rooms. Lots of activities. A great choice for the preschool set. Bring your own cake.

Laser Quest
3417 Plaza Drive
324-4800
Party rooms available. Especially popular with high-energy types. Bring your own cake.

Libertyland Amusement Park
940 Early Maxwell Boulevard
274-1776
Thrills and chills, all kinds of food, and entertainment. Party rooms and packages available.

MEMPHIS BROOKS MUSEUM OF ART

Bring your own cake. $100 non-refundable deposit.

Memphis Brooks Museum of Art
1934 Poplar Avenue
544-6200
Party room, arts and crafts with a staff professional. Great for the artistically inclined. Full catering available.

Memphis Pink Palace Museum
3050 Central Avenue
320-6320
Visit the Planetarium, take in an IMAX movie, check out the dinosaurs, or tour the latest traveling exhibit. Brother Juniper's can supply the food. Party room and packages available. Bring your own cake.

Memphis Zoo
2000 Prentiss Place
(in Overton Park)
276-WILD
The Zoo Rendezvous Room and the Picnic Pavilion are offered as part of three party packages that include cake, ice cream, and punch. Zoo rides are also available.

East Memphis

Billy Hardwick All Star Bowling Lanes
1576 S. White Station Road
683-2695
As a general rule, school-aged children love bowling parties. Snack bar and playroom on-site. Bring your own cake.

Benihana
912 Ridge Lake Blvd.
683-7390
Not inexpensive, but always fun. Will and his friends have loved celebrating birthdays here since they were in preschool. You get a tasty meal and live entertainment (those dexterous chefs!), all rolled into one. The restaurant also provides a modest but smile-producing birthday surprise at the end of the meal.

Build-a-Bear Workshop
Wolfchase Galleria
266-4548
www.buildabear.com
Kids can make their own stuffed animals. Free supplies for party guests. For details log onto the website and click on "build-a-party."

East End Skating Center
5718 Mt. Moriah
363-7785
It's loud and sometimes pretty crowded, but kids seem to love skating parties. East End provides birthday package deals, and private party rooms are on-site. Soft drinks, hot dogs, and other kid-friendly foods are available. Bring your own cake.

Embassy Suites Hotel
1022 S. Shady Grove Rd.
684-1777
We have had several "Sleep over and swim" parties here (with pizza delivery). Bring your own cake. Pricey, but always a hit.

Holiday Inn Express Hotel & Suites
4225 American Way
369-8005
Similar to the sleep-overs at Embassy Suites, but less expensive. Bring your own cake. Pizza deliveries welcome.

Lichterman Nature Center
5992 Quince Road
767-7322
www.memphismuseums.org
Party packages and private room available. Activities led by staff naturalist. Bring your own cake. Gift bags available through the Nature Gift Shop.

Malco Movie Theaters
15 Memphis area locations
681-2020 #128
www.malco.com
There are a couple of locations (Paradiso and Cordova) that offer birthday party packages 3 times a day, with a private party room and guaranteed seating. A party for 20 costs $210 ($50 for room rental and $8 a person for popcorn and drinks). For $100 you can rent an entire theater ($260 for 20 people) at any location, but only at 9 a.m. Bring your own cake and paper products.

Memphis Botanic Garden
750 Cherry Road
685-1566
www.memphisbotanicgarden.com
Mix fun, crafts, and activities with learning. Party room and staff host provided. Bring your own cake.

LICHTERMAN NATURE CENTER

Putt Putt Family Park
5484 Summer Avenue
386-2992
www.puttputtmemphis.com
Private party rooms available, plus pizza and beverages. Bring your own cake.

Seize the Clay
(Two locations)
5030 Poplar
683-2529
555 Perkins Rd. Ext.
683-5656
Children stick their fingers into soft squishy clay and leave with their own handmade pottery as a birthday souvenir.

South Memphis/Airport Area

Graceland
3734 Elvis Presley Blvd.
332-3322
The staff at Graceland can provide party rooms and a full range of services for both large and small parties (even weddings). It's the perfect place for a celebration with a true "Memphis touch."

MEMPHIS BOTANIC GARDEN

Helpful websites

General Information

City of Memphis:
www.cityofmemphis.org
Memphis Convention & Visitors Bureau:
www.memphistravel.com
Memphis Regional Chamber of Commerce:
www.memphischamber.com
Center City Commission:
www.downtownmemphis.com
Restaurants and menus:
www.memphismenus.com
www.memphisdining.com
City museum system:
www.memphismuseums.org
Memphis Symphony concerts for kids:
www.msokids.homestead.com
General entertainment:
www.memphismojo.com
www.jungleroom.com
City guides:
www.memphismemphis.com
www.memphisguide.com
LINC (Library Information Center):
725-8801
Food Xpress:
454-7223
(Deliveries from local restaurants to hotels & home)

Local Memphis Media
(partial listing)

Television:
WREG TV Channel 3 (CBS):
www.wreg.com
WMC TV Channel 5 (NBC):
www.wmcstations.com
WHBQ TV Channel 13 (FOX):
www.Fox13WHBQ.com
WPTY Channel 24 (ABC):
www.abc24.com
WLMT TV Channel 30 (UPN):
www.upn30memphis.com
WKNO TV Channel 10 (PBS):
www.wkno.org

Newspapers and magazines:

The Commercial Appeal:
www.gomemphis.com
Tri-State Defender:
523-1818

Mid-South Tribune:
728-5001
Best Times:
523-1561
Memphis Flyer:
www.memphisflyer.com
Memphis Magazine:
www.memphismagazine.com
Memphis Parent:
www.memphisparent.com
Memphis Business Journal:
www.bizjournals.com/memphis
The Daily News:
523-0936
Grace Magazine:
www.gracemagazine.com
The Downtowner Magazine:
www.memphisdowntowner.com
Key Magazine:
www.keymagazine.com/memphis
RSVP:
www.rsvpmagazine.com
LaPrensa Latina:
www.laprensalatina.com
Jabberblabber
(for creative kids):
www.jabberblabber.com

Regional tourism:

Tennessee State Department of Tourism:
www.tnvacation.com
Mississippi Division of Tourist Development:
www.visitmississippi.org
Arkansas State Department of Tourism:
www.Arkansas.com

Other tidbits

Movie Theaters
IMAX at the Pink Palace Museum:
763-IMAX
Hollywood 20 Cinema in Bartlett:
380-0900
Muvico at Peabody Place:
248-0100
Malco Theaters (15 locations):
681-2020
Malco Summer Quartet Drive-In:
767-4320

Central Library
3030 Poplar Avenue
415-2700

Memphis operates more than a dozen additional branches of the Memphis & Shelby County library system, but this is the largest and newest. A fine facility with lots of special programs aimed at young readers.

Babysitting Service:

Annie's Nannies Inc.
755-4533
I've used them several times. Nannies come to your home or hotel. Fully certified. A bit pricey, but very dependable. Sitters who are intelligent, warm, and friendly.

Medical Services

Le Bonheur Children's Medical Center
50 North Dunlap
Midtown/Medical Center
572-3000
Emergency Department
572-3112
Baptist Minor Medical Centers
2087 Union Avenue
274-3336
5030 Poplar Avenue
683-7937
6570 Stage Rd.
385-7817
4539 Winchester Rd.
227-0500
8066 Walnut Run Rd.
725-2900
584 N. Germantown Pkwy.
753-7686
350 N. Humphreys Blvd.
227-0483

AND FINALLY — some general travel info from around the web

www.roadsideamerica.com
(very off-beat attractions & news items)
www.familytravelforum.com
(travel planning for kids – excellent!)
www.eathere.com
(roadside diners)
www.festivalfinder.com
(music festivals)

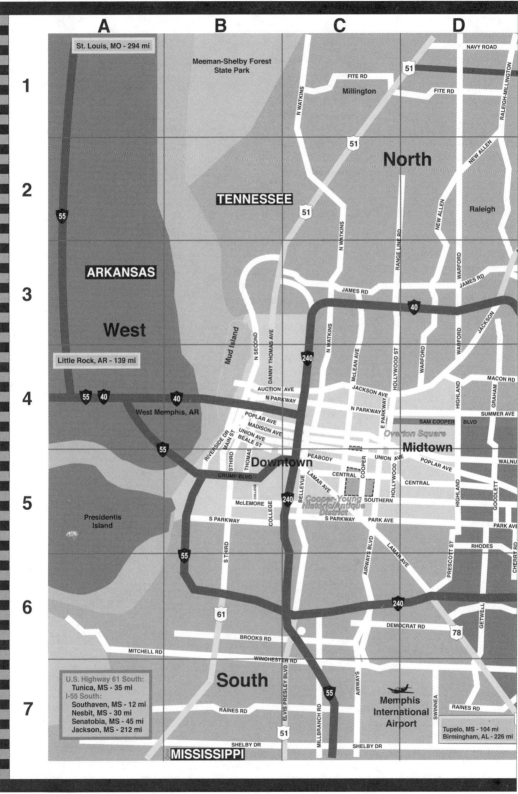

St. Louis, MO - 294 mi

Meeman-Shelby Forest State Park

FITE RD

Millington

FITE RD

NAVY ROAD

51

51

North

TENNESSEE

51

ARKANSAS

West

JAMES RD

40

James RD

JACKSON

Little Rock, AR - 139 mi

Mud Island

AUCTION AVE

N PARKWAY

55 40

40

West Memphis, AR

55

POPLAR AVE

MADISON AVE

UNION AVE

BEALE ST

Downtown

PEABODY

CENTRAL

SOUTHERN

Overton Square

Midtown

UNION AVE

POPLAR AVE

WALNU

CENTRAL

Presidentis Island

CRUMP BLVD

McLEMORE

S PARKWAY

240

Cooper-Young Historic/Antique District

S PARKWAY

PARK AVE

PARK AVE

55

AIRWAYS BLVD

LAMAR AVE

RHODES

CHERRY RD

61

BROOKS RD

240

DEMOCRAT RD

78

GETWELL

MITCHELL RD

WINCHESTER RD

South

U.S. Highway 61 South:
Tunica, MS - 35 mi
I-55 South:
Southaven, MS - 12 mi
Nesbit, MS - 30 mi
Senatobia, MS - 45 mi
Jackson, MS - 212 mi

RAINES RD

ELVIS PRESLEY BLVD

MILLBRANCH RD

AIRWAYS

55

SWINNEA

Memphis International Airport

RAINES RD

Tupelo, MS - 104 mi
Birmingham, AL - 226 mi

51

SHELBY DR

SHELBY DR

MISSISSIPPI

City Map

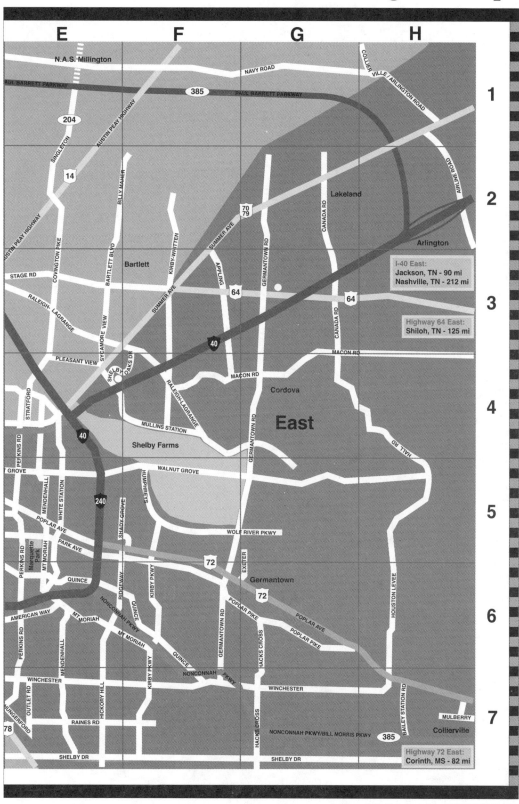

Acknowledgments

First and foremost, I must thank my patient and encouraging husband, Sledge, and our supportive offspring David, Andrew, and Will. If they had a nickel for every time I said, "I've got to work on the book," they could enjoy about a dozen years' worth of college tuition, plus a vacation home in the Caymans by now.

I also want to thank the Memphis Convention & Visitors Bureau (MCVB). This book would not have been possible without the knowledge and experience I gained as an employee there. More specifically, I am grateful to Kevin Kane for allowing me to include the MCVB's Memphis maps and to Ramona Rogers, the graphic designer and computer whiz who made them. My thanks, too, to Brian Johnston for the Memphis Music Timeline, to Patsy Morgan for her encyclopedic knowledge of attractions and events, and to my MCVB cheerleaders: Mary Schmitz, Alex Turner, and Andrea Perry.

I would be remiss if I did not express my sincere appreciation to one of my favorite people, Ramay Winchester, director of marketing for West Tennessee Heritage Tourism/Tennessee State Department of Tourist Development. He is a generous and delightful purveyor of information and assistance.

Additional thanks are in order to Amber Garrett at the Arkansas State Department of Tourism; Wilson Phillips, from Arlington; Rick and Debbie Pellicciotti of Belle Aire Biplane Tours; and thanks to Donna Taylor, who spent many hours on the telephone for me making new friends along the way.

To Headmaster Tom Beasley and Grace-St. Luke's Episcopal School: Thank you for letting me delay my starting date at the new job so I could spend my summer at my P.C.

In addition to my photographic efforts, photos were supplied by: the MCVB, Tennessee State Department of Tourist Development, Arkansas State Department of Tourism, Mississippi State Department of Tourism, Susan Wilson Hoggard, owner of the Wilson Hardware Store in Arlington, Debbie and Rick Pellicciotti at Belle Aire Biplane Tours, Amanda Dugger, and Hudd Byard.

Most importantly, I must pay homage to the many talented and dedicated folks at Contemporary Media for dressing up my ramblings and putting it in print. Specifically, my sincere thanks go to publisher Ken Neill and to my enthusiastic editor, Mary Helen Randall. We must do this again sometime! Thanks also to Jane Schneider, editor of *Memphis Parent*, for the seal of approval.

And, finally, to all my friends and family, and to the many total strangers who will, I'm sure, buy this book in mass quantities: Thank you! Please pay at the counter. All major credit cards accepted.

— Denise DuBois Taylor

Notes